100 WAI
Lincolnshire & Humberside

compiled by

HUGH MARROWS
&
GLEN HOOD

The Crowood Press

First published in 1996 by
The Crowood Press Ltd
Ramsbury
Marlborough
Wiltshire SN8 2HR

British Library Cataloguing-in-Publication Data
A catalogue record for this book is
available from the British Library

ISBN 1 86126 015 6

All maps by Janet Powell

Typeset by Carreg Limited, Ross-on-Wye, Herefordshire

Printed by J. W. Arrowsmith Limited, Bristol

CONTENTS

35.	Thorpe-on-the-Hill	$4\frac{1}{4}$m	$(6\frac{3}{4}$km)
36.	Stoke Rochford	$4\frac{1}{4}$m	$(6\frac{3}{4}$km)
37.	Holbeach Marsh	$4\frac{1}{2}$m	$(7\frac{1}{4}$km)
38.	Brinkhill and Warden Hill	$4\frac{1}{2}$m	$(7\frac{1}{4}$km)
39.	Tennyson Country	$4\frac{1}{2}$m	$(7\frac{1}{4}$km)
40.	Morton and Dyke	$4\frac{1}{2}$m	$(7\frac{1}{4}$km)
41.	Witham-on-the-Hill	$4\frac{1}{2}$m	$(7\frac{1}{4}$km)
42.	Haverholme and the Sleaford Canal	$4\frac{1}{2}$m	$(7\frac{1}{4}$km)
43.	Caistor and Nettleton	$4\frac{1}{2}$m	$(7\frac{1}{4}$km)
44.	Woodhall Spa	$4\frac{3}{4}$m	$(7\frac{1}{2}$km)
45.	Osbournby and the Tally Ho Inn	5m	(8km)
46.	Dunston and Wasps Nest	5m	(8km)
47.	Blankney and Scopwick	5m	(8km)
48.	Tetford and Ruckland	5m	(8km)
49.	… and longer version	$8\frac{1}{2}$m	$(13\frac{1}{2}$km)
50.	Well Vale and Ulceby	5m	(8km)
51.	Tathwell and Haugham	5m	(8km)
52.	Hainton and Sixhills	5m	(8km)
53.	Beverley and the Westwood	5m	(8km)
54.	Tophill Low Waters	5m	(8km)
55.	North Cave and Hotham	5m	(8km)
56.	Hull Bridge	5m	(8km)
57.	Keyingham	5m	(8km)
58.	Easington	5m	(8km)
59.	… and longer version	7m	$(11\frac{1}{4}$km)
60.	Branston	$5\frac{1}{4}$m	$(8\frac{1}{2}$km)
61.	Boston and the Haven	$5\frac{1}{4}$m	$(8\frac{1}{2}$km)
62.	The Theddlethorpes	$5\frac{1}{4}$m	$(8\frac{1}{2}$km)
63.	Stamford and Easton-on-the-Hill	$5\frac{1}{2}$m	$(8\frac{3}{4}$km)
64.	Marton and the Trent	$5\frac{1}{2}$m	$(8\frac{3}{4}$km)
65.	Barholm and Braceborough	$5\frac{1}{2}$m	$(8\frac{3}{4}$km)
66.	Irby Dales and Swallow	$5\frac{3}{4}$m	$(9\frac{1}{4}$km)
67.	Wold Newton and Beesby	6m	$(9\frac{1}{2}$km)
68.	Blankney Barff and the Car Dyke	6m	$(9\frac{1}{2}$km)
69.	Wellingore to Coleby	$6\frac{1}{2}$m	$(10\frac{1}{2}$km)
70.	Partney and Langton	$6\frac{1}{2}$m	$(10\frac{1}{2}$km)

71.	Hatcliffe, Cuxwold and Beelsby	7m	$(11^1/_4$km)
72.	Gedney Drove End	7m	$(11^1/_4$km)
73.	Bigby	7m	$(11^1/_4$km)
74.	Old Bolingbroke	$7^1/_4$m	$(11^1/_2$km)
75.	Louth and South Elkington	$7^1/_2$m	(12km)
76.	Crowland	$7^3/_4$m	$(12^1/_2$km)
77.	Burwell and Little Cawthorpe	8m	(13km)
78.	Corby Glen and Burton-le-Coggles	8m	(13km)
79.	Osbournby and Newton (Via Haceby)	8m	(13km)
80.	The Humber Bridge	8m	(13km)
81.	Tealby and Kirmond-le-Mire	8m	(13km)
82.	The Louth Canal and Alvingham	8m	(13km)
83.	Swayfield and Castle Bytham	8m	(13km)
84.	Barnoldby-le-Beck and Ravendale	8m	(13km)
85.	Warter	8m	(13km)
86.	Barmby on the Marsh	8m	(13km)
87.	Patrington	8m	(13km)
88.	Ingham to Glentworth	$8^3/_4$m	(14km)
89.	Caythorpe and Carlton Scoop	9m	$(14^1/_2$km)
90.	Burton Agnes and Rudston	9m	$(14^1/_2$km)
91.	Seaton	9m	$(14^1/_2$km)
92.	Kirby Underdale	9m	$(14^1/_2$km)
93.	Bardney and Southrey	$9^1/_4$m	$(14^3/_4$km)
94.	The Heath and Temple Bruer	$9^1/_2$m	$(15^1/_4$km)
95.	Epworth and Haxey	$9^1/_2$m	$(15^1/_4$km)
96.	Alkborough and West Halton	$9^3/_4$m	$(15^1/_4$km)
97.	Grimsthorpe Castle	10m	(16km)
98.	Biscathorpe and Burgh-on-Bain	10m	(16km)
99.	Nettleton and Rothwell	10m	(16km)
100.	Horncastle and Scrivelsby	$10^1/_2$m	(17km)

PUBLISHER'S NOTE

We very much hope that you enjoy the routes presented in this book, which has been compiled with the aim of allowing you to explore the area in the best possible way – on foot.

We strongly recommend that you take the relevant map for the area, and for this reason we list the appropriate Ordnance Survey maps for each route. Whilst the details and descriptions given for each walk were accurate at time of writing, the countryside is constantly changing, and a map will be essential if, for any reason, you are unable to follow the given route. It is good practice to carry a map and use it so that you are always aware of your exact location.

We cannot be held responsible if some of the details in the route descriptions are found to be inaccurate, but should be grateful if walkers would advise us of any major alterations. Please note that whenever you are walking in the countryside you are on somebody else's land, and we must stress that you should *always* keep to established rights of way, and *never* cross fences, hedges or other boundaries unless there is a clear crossing point.

Remember the country code:

Enjoy the country and respect its life and work
Guard against all risk of fire
Fasten all gates
Keep dogs under close control
Keep to public footpaths across all farmland
Use gates and stiles to cross field boundaries
Leave all livestock, machinery and crops alone
Take your litter home
Help to keep all water clean
Protect wildlife, plants and trees
Make no unnecessary noise

The walks are listed by length – from approximately 2 to 10 miles – but the amount of time taken will depend on the fitness of the walkers and the time spent exploring any points of interest along the way. Nearly all the walks are circular and most offer recommendations for refreshments.

Good walking.

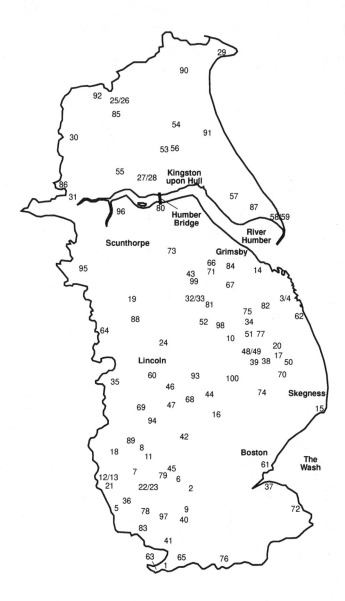

Walk 1   **A STAMFORD TOWN WALK**   1¹/₄m (2km)

Maps: OS Sheets Landranger 141; Pathfinder 897.

A brief look at a few of Stamford's historic buildings.

Start: At 028068, the car park in Station Road, Stamford.

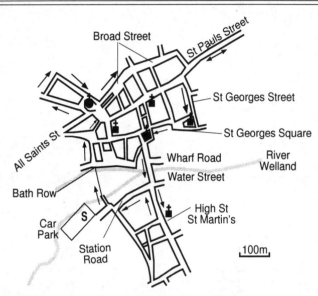

This short walk to see some (indeed only a fraction) of Stamford's immense heritage of old buildings can be added to the country walk to Easton (Walk 63) as it starts at the same car park.

From the car park entrance, turn left over a footbridge and walk across The Meadows towards the town. At the far side, cross another bridge and **Castle Dyke**. Walk ahead up to The Sheepmarket, cross and go up Horseshoe Lane (to the right of the Golden Fleece) into Red Lion Square. Keep left over All Saints' Place and continue along Scotgate. Just before the traffic lights, cross Scotgate to go up **Barn Hill** and, after a right turn at the top, descend to the back of All Saints' Place. Turn left into Crown Street: this becomes Broad Street, in which you pass **Browne's Hospital**, on the left. At the far end, turn into Star Lane, then go left along St Paul's Street, on the right of which can be found the **Brazenose Gate**.

Return down St Paul's Street, go left into St George's Street and right into St George's Square. Walk ahead into St Mary's Street, go left round St Mary's Square and then left down St Mary's Hill to cross the river and reach the **George Hotel**. In Station Road, on your right is the **Burghley Hospital**, but before returning to the car park, first make the effort to continue up High Street St Martin's. Looking back from here there is a marvellous view of the town, so little changed since J M W Turner made his famous painting of it.

POINTS OF INTEREST:

The Tourist Information Centre has several 'Town Trails'. Serious architecture 'students' might try reading Alec Clifton-Taylor's book *Six English Towns* which contains an essay on Stamford.

Virtually the whole route is lined with buildings of interest. Only a few, and none of the many magnificent churches, are singled out here. It was Stamford's unique buildings heritage that made it the first Conservation Area in 1967, and also drew the BBC to film much of the *Middlemarch* series here. George Eliot fans can try a little location spotting.

Castle Dyke – There was a Norman castle here though only three small arches remain. The bus station now perches on the castle mound.

Barn Hill – Even in Stamford this narrow road is strikingly picturesque. King Charles I spent his last night as a free man on 4th May 1646 in No. 9. Fleeing north in disguise, he later surrendered to the Scots.

Browne's Hospital – A fine medieval almshouse, built by a local wool merchant in 1475. It is sometimes open to the public.

Brazenose Gate – In 1333 disaffected students from Oxford made an attempt to found a rival university in Stamford. The gate dates from that time and the college, which lasted only three years, was nearby. The original knocker, the 'brazen nose', was returned to Oxford in 1890.

George Hotel – Although much altered over the years, the inn has existed since 1568, being a famous stopping place during the hey-day of stagecoaches. The beam above the road bearing the hotel sign was originally a gallows, meant to deter highwaymen.

Burghley Hospital – This was built by Lord Burghley in 1597, though there had been an earlier hospital on the same site.

REFRESHMENTS:

There is a wide selection in the town.

Walk 2   SEMPRINGHAM   2m (3¼km)

Maps: OS Sheets Landranger 130; Pathfinder 836.

A short, easy walk near the site of a 12th-century Gilbertine monastery.

Start: At 107329, Sempringham Church.

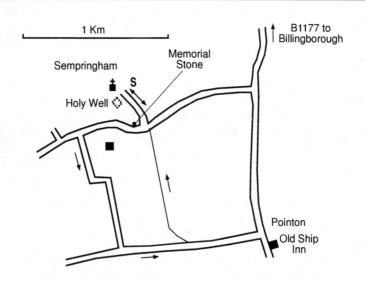

Just south of **Billingborough** a narrow lane turns off by an information board, heading across the fields to **Sempringham** priory church. Park at the lane end.

To add to the interest of the walk visit the churchyard before setting off. Near the south wall of the church, a three dimensional map describes the area and its history.

Walk back down the lane used to reach the start, but turn right along a track, by the **memorial stone**, before the bridge. Walk with a stream on your left until you reach a sleeper bridge, also on the left. Cross this bridge and take the uphill track ahead, following it as it bends left, then right, before descending to reach a road at the edge of Pointon village.

Turn left and, after entering Pointon, look for a kissing gate and a footpath sign on the left, at the corner of a small paddock before the second house. Cross the paddock diagonally left to reach a footbridge at the far side. Take the headland path a few feet to your right, going uphill by a small lone tree. At the top, from a narrow bridge over a ditch, the way is clear ahead, heading back down a grassy headland to join the lane leading to the church. Now take the last few steps back to the start.

POINTS OF INTEREST:

Billingborough – Although not on the route, the village is worth visiting. There are many interesting houses and a charming short walk, in the back lanes away from the main road, by the Spring Wells near the church. At weekends there is a marvellous 'glory hole' of a second-hand book shop in the High Street.

Sempringham – The village, which has disappeared, was situated to the north-west of the church. The church now stands alone, but because it is on a rise looks strangely proud and impressive, remaining in sight through much of the walk. St Gilbert was born here (about 1083). The son of a nobleman, he was born deformed and was not thought suited to the life of a knight. Nevertheless he lived to be over 100. The Gilbertine order which he founded, was the only monastic order to have been founded in this country. Unusually, it admitted both men and women, though they occupied separate accommodation. The church has much Norman work. Near the bottom of the churchyard is a small Holy Well. For an inspection of the church the key has to be fetched from Pointon.

The Memorial Stone – The stone commemorates Gwenllian, daughter of the Prince of Wales, who was imprisoned at Sempringham for 54 years until she died in 1337. Compare this date with that of her birth!

REFRESHMENTS:

None en route, but the following are close by:

The Old Ship Inn, Pointon.

The Fortescue Arms, Billingborough.

The George and Dragon, Billingborough.

There are also inns in nearby Horbling and Threekingham, as well as inns and tea-rooms in Folkingham.

SALTFLEET HAVEN   2m ($3\frac{1}{4}$km)
or 7m ($11\frac{1}{4}$km)

Maps: OS Sheets Landranger 113; Pathfinder 732.

A varied walk on the sea marshes and inland.

Start: At 456934, the car park at the southern end of Saltfleet.

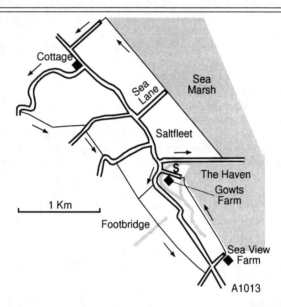

Approaching **Saltfleet** from the south the car park is on the right at the first left-hand bend, before crossing the Haven. It is called Paradise!

The short walk turns left out of the car park: follow the main road (the A1031), with care, to its first left-hand bend and go up the lane ahead for 300 yards. A path comes over a footbridge from the right. This is the longer route joining the shorter version.

The longer route turns right out of the car park, crossing the **Haven** and turning right again along a track. About 100 yards beyond a car park and picnic site (at grid reference 463935), turn left along the marsh edge. Keep forward to reach a concrete ramp giving access to Sea Lane (nearby is a large MOD notice board: can you find the spelling mistake?). Stay on the sea marsh for a further 1,000 yards to reach a small creek

12

near a circular MOD warning sign. Turn inland (through a car park at grid reference 448952) and walk to a road. Turn left, then take the first lane on the right, near a cottage, signed as a 'No Through Road'. The lane becomes unsurfaced before veering left, then very sharply right, to reach the bank of the Sunderfleet Eau. Turn left and walk to a road. A short distance to the right a grassy lane goes off to the left by a wide drain: follow this to the next road. Walk ahead along the road to reach a white house and take the path along its left side, rejoining the drain by walking along the field edge to reach a footbridge. Cross the bridge to rejoin the shorter route.

Maintain direction until a wide drain is reached. Now go right for a few yards (there is a bridge!) and return along the other side. Resume your original direction to reach another bridge on the left. Cross to reach a road. Turn left and go over at the crossroads to reach the sand dunes beyond Sea View Farm. (There is yet another car park here, at grid reference 464924). Turn left along the marsh edge again. Cross a bridge on the left and follow the track beyond back to Paradise.

POINTS OF INTEREST:
Saltfleet and the Haven – It is hard to imagine today, but the Haven was a bustling medieval port, and was required to supply ships and men at times of national emergency. Large areas of the dunes and foreshore south of the village are a Nature Reserve, a rare inhabitant of which is the natterjack toad. You are on the Reserve during the latter part of the walk. Much of the charm of the area is the wonderful skyscapes, both over the sea marsh, and inland across the miles of flat fields towards the Wolds.

REFRESHMENTS:
The New Inn, Saltfleet.
The Crown Inn, Saltfleet.
The Prussian Queen, is 2 miles to the south at grid reference 453908.
During the summer teas are served in the redundant church of Saltfleetby St Clement, just off the route at grid reference 459918. There is also a seasonal fish and chip shop at the seaward end of Sea Lane, only a 'stone's throw' away as you march along the beach.

Walk 5   **SKILLINGTON**   2m (3$^1/_4$km)

Maps: OS Sheets Landranger 130; Pathfinder 855.

A short walk near a village with an unusual historic association.

Start: At 898257, the green in front of Skillington Wesleyan chapel.

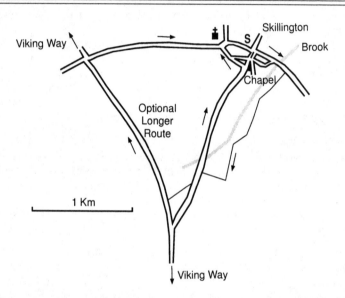

Walk downhill away from the chapel and turn right beyond the Crossed Swords Inn. Just beyond the bridge over the Cringle Brook cross a stile on the right.

The route now lies over meadows opened to the public through the Countryside Commission's Stewardship Scheme. The brook valley is marshy and important for its plants, herbs and other wildlife.

Keep forward, contouring across the first field above the brook, then bearing down to the right to cross a footbridge. Go left to continue up the valley, going past a pond and over a second footbridge. Where the brook veers off to the right, go left under some electricity wires, then bear right up the slope of the field to reach a stile. Go straight across the field beyond to reach an unmetalled lane (Buckminster Lane).

Turn right and walk back to **Skillington**. At the edge of the village, take the first lane on the left and follow it around to the small green to visit the church. A further right turn leads back to the start.

Those who would like a slightly longer walk – $4^1/_4$m (7km) – can turn left on reaching Buckminster Lane. In a few steps a path on the right goes over a field to reach the Viking Way. Turn right to reach a road, where another right turn will bring you back to the village by the church.

POINTS OF INTEREST:

Skillington – An attractive village of stone houses and farms. The large trees are subject to preservation orders and this helps to maintain the charm. An imposing Wesleyan chapel of 1847 dominates the centre. The remains of a medieval cross are on another small green by the church.

It is the church of St James itself which holds the real interest however, for it had a most unusual vicar in the 1860s. The Rev. Charles Hudson was a leading amateur mountaineer of his day and after having climbed Mont Blanc and Monte Rosa he joined the famous alpinist Edward Whymper in his attempt to make the first ascent of the Matterhorn. A party of seven set out on 13th July 1865 and reached the summit on the following day. On the descent, however, a fall by one of the party dragged three others, including Hudson, to their deaths. Whymper and two guides survived. Two stained glass windows in the church commemorate Hudson, both showing the distinctive outline of the mountain. The larger one bears a list of fellow mountaineers who subscribed to its cost, including Whymper himself.

REFRESHMENTS:
The Blue Horse, Skillington.
The Crossed Swords, Skillington.

Walk 6   **FOLKINGHAM** $2^1/_4$m ($3^1/_2$km)

Maps: OS Sheets Landranger 130; Pathfinder 836.

The village that is an architecture lover's delight.

Start: At 072336, Folkingham Market Place.

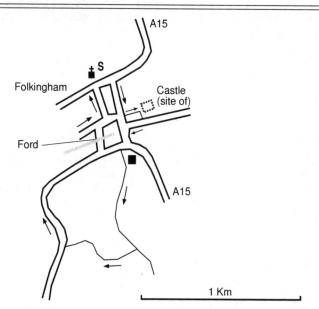

Park at the top of the wide Market Place in **Folkingham** and walk downhill along the right-hand side until you are opposite the filling station. Cross the road and take the short footpath from the back left-hand corner of the forecourt. Cross a lane and climb a stile into a field adjacent to the **old castle** site. Bear slightly right, walk past the moat and down to another stile at the road near the entrance to the **House of Correction**. Turn right to reach the main road again.

Cross, with care, and go left along the pavement for 100 yards. Turn right into Greenfields Lane and, almost immediately, take the footpath by the two metal gates on the left. Pass to the right of a bungalow and walk straight down the field to a reach a gateway in a hedge. Go through, turn right, and keeping fairly close to the hedge and stream on your right, continue to a stile in the field corner. Cross and walk forward to join a track.

Turn right and follow the track, through a double bend, until it joins a wide, hedged green lane. Now turn right again and follow the lane to reach a metalled lane. This is Greenfields Lane again.

Go left, downhill, cross the ford by a footbridge, and turn right at the corner by the entrance to a caravan site. Take the next road on the left - Chapel Lane - and, at the top, bear right into West Street to return to the Market Place.

POINTS OF INTEREST:

Folkingham – Uncharacteristically this village is spread along a hilltop, looking particularly impressive from the south. It has a wealth of interesting buildings surrounding its wide Market Place, with the church and the 18th-century coaching inn, the Greyhound, dominating the top of the hill. This was once used as the Sessions House. Lower down on the left is the three-storeyed Manor House, built in the mid-17th century, and around the corner from the church in West Street is the Workhouse of 1813 with an enormous overhanging roof. An architectural oddity of the locality is a moustache-shaped window lintel, several of which can be seen in the Market Place. There are similar lintels in the surrounding villages.

The Castle and House of Correction – Only the moat now remains of the castle, originally Norman, which was recorded as becoming ruinous as long ago as 1535. On its site was built the House of Correction, dated 1825, though only the governor's house-cum-gatehouse is now left. It belongs to the Landmark Trust and can be rented for holidays.

REFRESHMENTS:

The New Inn, Folkingham.
The Whipping Post, Folkingham.
There are also other refreshment opportunities in Folkingham.

Walk 7   **LONDONTHORPE** $2^{1}/_{2}$m (4km)

Maps: OS Sheets Landranger 130; Pathfinder 835.

A walk near the beautiful surroundings of the National Trust's Belton Park.

Start: At 940390, a free National Trust car park below the folly at Bellmount.

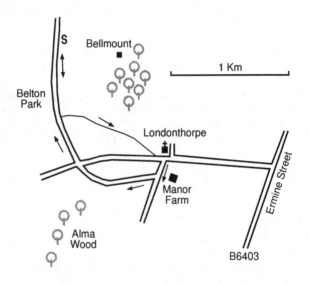

Perhaps the easiest access to the start is to turn off Ermine Street (the B6403) into **Londonthorpe**. Once through the village take the lane on the right at the bottom of the hill.

Turn left from the car park entrance, going along the lane for 400 yards to reach a stile on the left. Go over this and aim for Londonthorpe church, seen on the hill, crossing a grass field to reach another stile near a gate. Beyond this, go through a high gate into an area of protected young woodland and bear left to reach a second high gate and a stile. In the next field, head half-right towards a long house to the right of the church. After crossing a third stile, continue uphill towards the same house: a small metal gate in the field corner gives access to the road.

A short detour up the road to the left leads to the church. This detour is recommended, both for the church itself and because the churchyard is one of several vantage points in the village for far reaching views over the valley and **Belton Park**.

Return to the metal gate and walk up Newgate Lane opposite. After 100 yards, take the unsurfaced track off to the right, following it downhill. An option to extend this part of the walk is provided by the Woodland Trust, whose notice boards extend an invitation to explore Alma Wood on the left.

When Newgate Lane reaches a road, the lane opposite leads directly back to the start.

POINTS OF INTEREST:

Londonthorpe – Perched on the skyline (it almost looks like Italy) this estate village is kept immaculately and has won awards from the Council for the Preservation of Rural England. The church has an unusual saddleback tower. If locked, an easy inspection can be made through the windows. As it is sunk into the hillside the view inside is as from a balcony. Apart from the beautiful stone houses and cottages, look for the village fountain.

Belton Park – Belton House is one of England's great country houses, built in the 17th century and now a National Trust property. It has both a magnificent interior and beautiful gardens. The BBC TV Serial *Moondial* was filmed here.

The House is surrounded by the beautiful deer park which is overlooked by the Bellmount Tower, from the top of an avenue of trees leading down to the House. The Tower was built in 1750 for Lord Tyrconnel and was restored by the National Trust in 1989. You can walk up to it from the car park.

On the walk you may notice waymarkers for the 'Gingerbread Way'. This is a 25 mile walk around Grantham, inaugurated for the Golden Jubilee of the Ramblers Association. Gingerbreads are Grantham's local delicacy.

REFRESHMENTS:

None en route, but there are plenty of facilities in Grantham 3 miles away. There is also a tea-room in the converted stables at Belton House.

Walk 8   **ANCASTER** $2^1/_2$m (4km)

Maps: OS Sheets Landranger 130; Pathfinder 814.

A short level walk from a Roman town, with lakes and birdlife.

Start: At 983436, Ancaster Church.

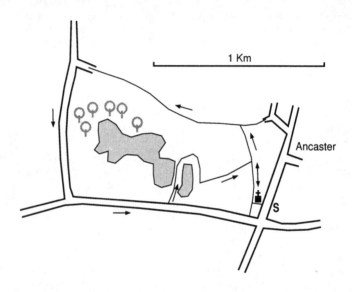

There is room to park on the road by the church gate. Walk 11, which follows The Valley near **Ancaster**, also starts here. Together they make a good figure of eight route.

From the gate walk through the churchyard and turn right along the lane behind it. Ignore a footpath joining on the left. Beyond some bungalows the marshy area to the left (Moor Closes) is a Nature Reserve. At a track junction, turn left to reach a metal gate. Now veer half-right, staying with the track to reach a road – Rookery Lane.

Turn left and walk past Moor Plantation. The lakes come into view here. Continue to reach the main A153. Turn left, with care, and, after 800 yards, just beyond the garage, turn left again along a footpath. In places the path is close to the water's edge, so keep an eye on children and pets! Walk forward between the two lakes, the one on the right being much the smaller. Follow the path as it curves around to the far side of the smaller lake and, just beyond the last island, look for a gap in the hedge on the left. Go through and cross the narrow field beyond to reach a stile.

Cross and walk with a wire fence on your left, then head towards two electricity poles near a bungalow. Do not be tempted to aim for the church: even though this is clearly seen and your eventual destination. Near the electricity poles there is a stile: cross and turn right to return to the church. The notice on the gate to the **cemetery** will interest botanists.

POINTS OF INTEREST:

Ancaster – The lakes on Willoughby Moor are privately owned by an angling club. However, it is possible to see most of them from the right of way. There are numerous points from which the wide variety of waterfowl they support can be observed. Have binoculars in your rucksack. See, also, the Note to Walk 11.

Ancaster Cemetery – This is a Site of Special Scientific Interest. According to a notice on the gate, it is one of only two sites in Britain where Tall Thrift grows. Whilst botanists will be delighted, the layman must surely wonder how they know this to be true! The plant is related to the Thrift (Sea Pink) common on coastal cliffs.

REFRESHMENTS:

The Ermine Way Inn, Ancaster.

The Railway Inn, Ancaster – at the north end of the village.

There is also a fish and chip shop and the lakeside provides a good picnic spot.

Walk 9   **DUNSBY AND HACONBY** $2^3/_4$m ($4^1/_2$km)

Maps: OS Sheets Landranger 130; Pathfinder 856.

A short easy walk on the fringe of the fens.

Start: At 106268, just east of Dunsby church.

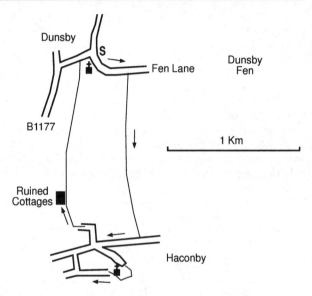

In **Dunsby** there is room to park (with care) at the main road junction with Fen Lane.

Walk down Fen Lane to reach a stile on the right opposite White House. Cross this and two further stiles very close together, and then, in a further 50 yards, go right at a gate into a large grass field. Turn half-left across the field to reach a fieldgate by a large fallen tree. Go through the gate and, aiming just left of **Haconby** church, cross an arable field to reach another stile and a footbridge. Cross these and, with a ditch to your right, continue to the road in Haconby village.

Turn right along the road to reach a footpath on the left by the old Baptist Chapel. Follow this path behind some cottages. Where the path divides, keep left (there is a profusion of waymarkers here) to reach a fingerpost at a stile. Cross and go half-right to reach a second stile into a paddock. Go forward to reach a third stile on the far side. Cross and turn very sharply to the right, following a wire fence to the corner of the churchyard. Go ahead beside the wall, following a green track to a lane corner.

Turn right and at the next corner, near the inn, turn right again. After 200 yards, near the pond, go left along a byway. Go through a fieldgate and bear right around a hedge corner. Now aim for the ruined cottages at the far left-hand corner of the field. Cross the double stile by a gate and walk directly towards Dunsby church. There is another stile in the hedge ahead. Cross and walk straight out from this (i.e. to the left of your direct line to Dunsby) to reach a footbridge across a dyke. Now resume your direct line, passing a pond to reach another stile. Cross the large pasture field beyond, still heading for the church. In the far right corner of this field there is a stile near a gate. Cross and continue to a (final) stile just beyond. Cross on to a road and turn right back to the start.

POINTS OF INTEREST:

Dunsby – This is one of a string of villages set where the land begins to rise from the vast empty fenlands to the east. The church is mostly 14th-century, and so are the scant remains of a medieval cross on the corner where Fen Lane leaves the main road. (Mind you don't trip over it!)

Haconby – The village, which has Danish origins, has a fine church and several old houses. The atmosphere in the meadows by the stone Manor House with its pond, geese and grazing animals is pure Middle Ages. The 17th-century Hacconby Hall (to your left as you join the road after passing the church) was once the home of General Fynne, an aide-de-camp to Oliver Cromwell.

REFRESHMENTS:

The Sportsman Inn, Haconby.

Walk 10   **GOULCEBY AND RED HILL**   3m (5km)
Maps: OS Sheets Landranger 122; Pathfinder 766 and 748.
Wonderful Wolds scenery and a Nature Reserve.
Start: At 254791, the Three Horseshoes Inn car park.

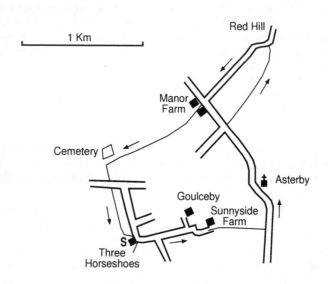

Parking is by kind permission of the inn landlord, so please park considerately.

Turn right out of the car park into **Goulceby**. Go straight on at the road junction and, after a further 200 yards, ignore a lane to the left, continuing along a 'No Through Road'. Ignore two signed footpaths (one on the left and one on the right), continuing to Sunnyside Farm beyond the double bend. Go into the farmyard and cross the stile at the far side. Walk across the large grass field beyond to its far right-hand corner. Cut through the hedge on your right and then continue ahead, with the hedge now on your left. Cross two more stiles, climb a grass bank and skirt left around a reservoir to reach a road.

Turn left along the road, following it for about 1,000 yards, and passing Asterby church, now redundant and privately owned, to reach a lane on the left signed to Goulceby. Take the footpath on the right opposite this lane, climbing gradually at first, then steeply, to emerge on to a road near the top of **Red Hill**.

After exploring the Nature Reserve that tops the hill, and admiring the view, walk downhill (westwards) along the road. At the T-junction, cross straight over and go through Manor Farm. Go through two gates and continue ahead along a grass track, crossing a pasture and two stiles. Ignore a signed footpath to the left and, at a third stile, cross into the old Goulceby cemetery. At the far side, turn left along a wide green lane, part of the Viking Way, a National Trail.

Where the lane meets a road, cross and walk ahead down a path which is sometimes a bit overgrown. After 100 yards, climb the stile on the left and at once turn right down a long grass field. Look for a waymarker on the fence away to your left, then bear left to reach a road. Turn right to return to the Three Horseshoes.

POINTS OF INTEREST:

Goulceby – A secluded village tucked away in the Wolds south-west of Louth. The church is both new and old, having been built only in 1908, but using the materials of the old one.

Red Hill – Acknowledged as one of the best view points in this part of the Wolds, Red Hill has for some years been a Nature Reserve managed by the Lincolnshire Trust for Nature Conservation. Originally a quarry, its name and its striking appearance are due to the unusual geological feature of red chalk, that is chalk coloured by iron when the underwater deposits from which it was formed were laid down in the Cretaceous period between 135 and 65 million years ago. The area supports a wide range of chalk loving plants including vetches and orchids. It is also a haunt of many varieties of butterfly. An information board gives detailed descriptions of what to look out for. On a fine day it is a fabulous picnic spot too!

REFRESHMENTS:
The Three Horseshoes Inn, Goulceby.

Walk 11   THE VALLEY, ANCASTER   3m (5km)

Maps: OS Sheets Landranger 130; Pathfinder 814.

A short walk from an ancient Roman settlement on the Ermine Street.

Start: At 983436, Ancaster Church.

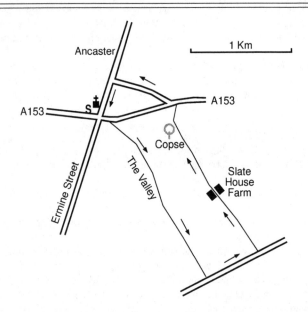

The road at the church is wide enough to permit easy parking. This second walk in **Ancaster** starts at the same point as Walk 8 and the two can be combined, as a figure of eight, to make a pleasant and easy day. A very short stretch of main road is unavoidable near the start.

Walk back to the crossroads with the A153 and turn left for 50 yards. Now cross, with great care, to enter **The Valley**. At a gate (and a Nature Reserve sign) keep left up a rising, tree-lined bridleway to reach another gate. (A path drops steeply to the right from here, a further right turn along the valley bottom providing an even shorter circular route.) Go through the gate and walk with a hedge on your left to reach a road.

Turn left and walk along the road to reach a footpath sign at the entrance to Slate House Farm. Take the farm road, not the path, leftwards over a field, then walk between the farm buildings and continue with a hedge on your right. Where the hedge ends, go half-left towards a small copse, then follow the headland down to reach the A153 again.

Cross, again with great care, and walk down the lane opposite into Ancaster. Turn left to return to the church.

POINTS OF INTEREST:

Ancaster – The Roman road known as Ermine Street ran from London to Stamford, and thence to Lincoln and north to the Humber. Ancaster was a fort and town on this major highway. The area was previously occupied in the Iron Age however, and there is a large prehistoric hill fort above Honington, 2 miles to the south-west. Ermine Street forms the main village street. The Roman town spanned this, but the main part was opposite the church. Many remains and artefacts have been found, a horde of 2000 coins on one occasion. It is said the locals used Roman coins as currency 200 years ago.

Fame also attends the local quarries where a beautiful limestone is found. Its special feature is that it hardens on exposure to the atmosphere. It has had extensive use throughout the area. Examples immediately to hand are Ancaster Church and The Hall, close to the start, with its unusual stone balustrade between the road and the pavement.

The Valley – A natural feature and local beauty spot. Formed in the local Jurassic limestone, it is well known for its lime loving plants, including some orchids, and is managed as a nature reserve by the Lincolnshire Trust for Nature Conservation.

REFRESHMENTS:

The Ermine Way Inn, Ancaster.
The Railway Inn, Ancaster – at the north end of the village.
There is also a fish and chip shop in Ancaster.

Maps: OS Sheets Landranger 130; Pathfinder 835.
Varied terrain and varied views.
Start: At 843351, the Dirty Duck Inn — by permission of the landlord.

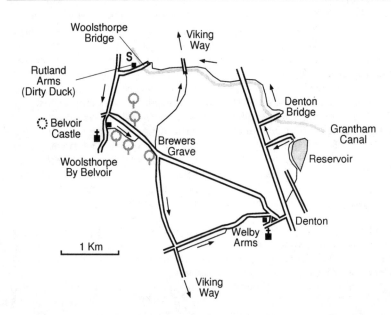

Walk back to the road and turn left towards Woolsthorpe By Belvoir village, passing the stables of the famous Belvoir Hunt near the cross-roads. There are good views of **Belvoir Castle** from here. Keep straight on at the crossroads and then turn left along a lane by the Chequers Inn. You are now on the **Jubilee Way**. At the rear of the inn, walk up the cricket field to a stile behind the pavilion. Cross and go steeply uphill. As the ground levels, veer left towards some woods and a waymarked gate on your left. Follow a track from here to a road. Turn right and walk to a bend where the Viking Way crosses the road. This is **Brewers Grave**.

The short walk turns left here, following the Viking Way as it descends with striking views of the Vale of Belvoir. The Way reaches a bridge over the Grantham Canal (*see* Note to Walk 21). Cross and turn left rejoining the longer route.

The longer walk turns right along **Sewstern Lane** (also following the Viking Way) for 1 mile to reach a road. Cross, but immediately turn left along a signed footpath, following the headland path as it runs parallel to the road to reach a stile at a wall. Cross and turn right along the road beyond to Denton. Keep right at a junction, then take a lane on the right to reach the Welby Arms and the church. Now with your back to the inn walk to your left, through the village, to reach a T-junction. Turn left and, shortly, take a path to the right, going over a series of stiles to reach a reservoir. Ignore a footbridge on the right, skirting the reservoir in a clockwise direction. At the far end, near a lifebelt, go left down a ramp to join a track. Turn left and follow the track to a road. Turn right for 300 yards, then turn right down another track. Cross the bridge at the canal, where there is a picnic site. Turn left along the canal towpath, rejoining the short route at another footbridge.

Follow the towpath back to the start.

POINTS OF INTEREST:

Belvoir Castle– The castle is actually just over the border in Leicestershire. The castle - whose name means 'beautiful view' – was first built in Norman times by Robert de Todeni, one of the Conqueror's supporters. It has been rebuilt several times over the centuries, the last time being after a fire in 1816. It is the ancestral home of the Dukes of Rutland.

The Jubilee Way – The walk between Woolsthorpe and Brewers Grave is the final section of a waymarked path from Melton Mowbray which links with the Viking Way.

Brewers Grave– It is reputedly just that! – marking the resting place of a castle brewer who drowned in his own vat.

Sewstern Lane– The lane follows the line of a prehistoric trackway, one of the oldest routes in Lincolnshire. By the time you leave it to head for Denton it has become the county boundary with Leicestershire.

REFRESHMENTS:

The Rutland Arms, Woolsthorpe. The inn, situated on the once-busy wharf and formerly a canal boatmen's inn, has two names. Its signboard shows both Rutland Arms and Dirty Duck, the latter being much better known and even being used for the telephone directory entry.

The Chequers, Woolsthorpe By Belvoir.

The Welby Arms, Denton.

Walk 14   **TETNEY LOCK**   3m (5km)

Maps: OS Sheets Landranger 113; Pathfinder 720.

A walk on Tetney Haven bank to panoramic views of the Humber estuary.

Start: At 342023, opposite the converted chapel, Tetney Lock.

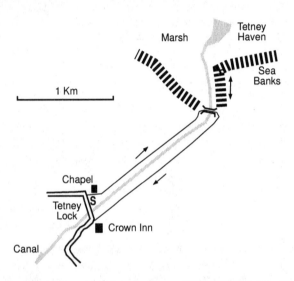

Tetney Lock is 2 miles east of Tetney village and the A1031. Parking is straightforward near the bend 200 yards north of the Crown Inn. There is a wide variety of birdlife to be seen both on the canal and on the marsh. The described walk is short, but two extensions are suggested.

Walk away from the road on the bank, with Tetney Drain to your right. This shortly joins the wider Louth Navigation Canal. Continue along the bank top to reach a farm track, then follow the track to reach a bridge.

Cross to the far bank, turn left and climb the stile to the left of a gate. Continue out towards the estuary until the bank turns sharply to the right. There is a good view from here, taking in the **Humber Estuary**, Spurn Point lighthouse and the **Haile Sand** and **Bull Sand Forts**. (It is possible to walk considerably further if you wish.)

Retrace your steps to the sluice, re-cross the stile, but this time return to **Tetney Lock** on the other bank to emerge on the road in front of the Crown Inn. Turn right over the bridge to reach the start, 200 yards way.

Other canal side walks follow both banks over meadows in the opposite direction. One starts on the right, 100 yards down the road from the inn, the other begins at the end of the lane, opposite the telephone box. However, the first obvious crossing point is at a bridge on a private farm road.

POINTS OF INTEREST:

Humber Estuary – Although it can look close on a clear day Spurn Point lighthouse is in fact 5 miles away across this massive estuary which drains one fifth of England's river water. Large ports upstream at Grimsby, Immingham, Hull and Goole ensure that there is always plenty of shipping to watch.

Haile Sand and Bull Sand Forts – These were built in 1915-1918 to protect the estuary from submarines. They are constructed of concrete and armoured steel cladding.

Tetney Lock – This is the seaward end of the Louth Navigation Canal. Twelve miles long, it was authorised in 1763 and completed in 1770. The cost was £28,000. Apart from Tetney Lock there were 6 others, all in the last 3 miles to Louth. It was last used in 1924.

REFRESHMENTS:

The Crown Inn, Tetney Lock.

The Plough, Tetney, 2 miles to the east.

There are also inns in the nearby villages of North Cotes and Marshchapel.

Maps: OS Sheets Landranger 122; Pathfinder 800.

An easy stroll around the sandhills and beach of the Nature Reserve.

Start: At 556581, the Nature Reserve car park.

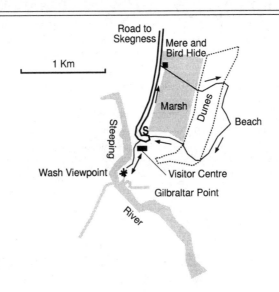

The **Nature Reserve** has a Visitor Centre at the car park and a visit to this is strongly recommended before the walk. Do carry binoculars. There is a small fee for parking.

Leave the car park at the opposite end to the Visitor Centre and walk straight ahead past a concrete wartime pill-box. At Post No. 13, go left up a grass bank and turn right along the top, following a wide grassy track which runs parallel to the marsh edge. This, and the lower path, converge at the approach to the **Mere** and the bird observation hide.

    On leaving the hide, turn left along a stony track. Just before a sleeper path up on to the dunes, turn left along a grass path which, after about 300 yards, gradually veers right on to the dune tops. Here, double back sharply to the right to reach a fenced viewpoint known as **Mill Hill**. Take the stone path down leftwards to reach the beach and turn right along the tideline.

As the dune ridge sweeps inland, follow it, passing sleeper steps on to the dunes and Post No. 7. Continue until a small hut is reached (if you go too far along the foreshore you will see this hut inland to your right - retrace your steps a short way or you will have an area of mud to cross). Pass behind the hut and walk along the saltmarsh edge. A 'No Unauthorised Access' sign is soon reached: turn right over the dunes by the **Bird Ringing Centre** and laboratory. From the front of the centre, bear right again and then go left along a wide track back to the start.

At the car park, continue past the Visitor Centre, following the picturesque creek of the Steeping River to the **Wash Viewpoint** (reached after about 400 yards). Then, finally, return to your car.

POINTS OF INTEREST:

Gibraltar Point Nature Reserve – The reserve covers 1,000 acres of dunes, marsh, grasslands and ponds and is managed by the Lincolnshire Trust for Nature Conservation. The Visitor Centre has visual displays and literature to explain the evolution of the area, what there is to see (in terms of landscape and wildlife) and the Trust's conservation work. A visit here first will do much to enhance the enjoyment of your walk. There are also information boards around the Reserve and a numbered nature trail.

The Mere – This was excavated in 1972/73 and is subject to controlled flooding to attract wildfowl. A wide variety of birds can usually be seen from the public hide.

Mill Hill – Though of modest height, the hill gives a tremendous all-round view. To appreciate how rapidly the marsh and dunes develop remember that the old Coastguard House (by the Visitor Centre) was on the coast when it was built in 1859. Seals can sometimes be seen on the sandbanks in the Wash and the Norfolk coast is visible.

The Bird Ringing Centre – A netting tunnel allows birds to be caught and ringed in order to study migration patterns etc.

Wash Viewpoint – From here there are wide ranging views over the marshes. Hulks on the skyline are targets for RAF bombing practice and aircraft can often be seen performing aerobatics over them. A painted panorama on the walls inside identifies features to be seen. It was opened by the broadcaster Julian Pettifer in 1986.

REFRESHMENTS:

There are none en route, but Skegness, with a wealth of inns, cafés etc, is only a few minutes away.

Walk 16   TATTERSHALL AND CONINGSBY   3m (5km)

Maps: OS Sheets Landranger 122; Pathfinder 799.

Part country walk, part village walk, this route visits sites of widely contrasting historic interest.

Start: At 212579, Tattershall Market Place.

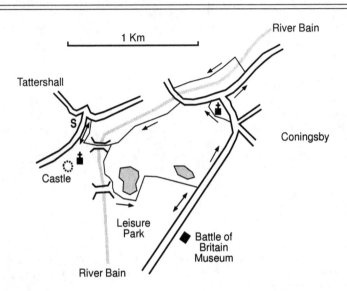

Tattershall Castle is a National Trust property. Members and visitors can park there. The car park (at grid reference 213577) is passed on the walk.

Cross the road in front of the Fortescue Arms to visit **Tattershall College**. Now turn left and, after 50 yards, take the path on the left. Go over a footbridge - the 'ditch' beneath is the remains of the canal to Horncastle. You are now in the National Trust car park. **Tattershall Castle** and **Church** can be reached by crossing the car park and turning right.

To continue the walk turn left, cross the River Bain by footbridge and go right, along the riverbank. At a girder bridge, turn left to walk past a lake. Go left behind it, then right on a path to reach a road. Turn right to visit the **Battle of Britain Memorial Flight** Museum.

Retrace your steps and walk into the village. Keep forward at a road junction, but take a path on the left by the Community Hall and opposite the quaint shops at No. 47/49. Turn right by the school to reach **Coningsby Church**. Leave by the gate beyond the tower and turn right along the road. Cross carefully at the zebra crossing just after the T-junction and continue walking away from the church. Just before the Black Swan, go left into Masons Lane. Beyond a footbridge, take the riverside path on the left to reach a road. Cross, turn left, then right: the riverside path continues, but on the opposite bank. At the footbridge, rejoin the outward route, reversing it to return to the start.

POINTS OF INTEREST:

Tattershall College – The church and castle were built by Ralph, Lord Cromwell (Lord Treasurer to Henry the Sixth), the church being founded in 1438 and the castle begun about 1455. They were served by a community of priests who lived in a 'college'. These remains may have been both school and living quarters.

Tattershall Castle – One of the best medieval brick buildings in the country, it had fallen almost into ruin by the early 1900s. It was restored by Lord Curzon and presented to the National Trust. It is now possible to climb the 181 steps to the roof and turrets, admiring the increasingly complex and decorative internal brickwork as you ascend. The dungeons are beneath the 20 feet thick walls.

Tattershall Church – An amazingly light building, its spaciousness enhanced by enormous windows of clear glass. Lord Cromwell did not see his church finished: it was completed after his death by Bishop William of Wayneflete who also founded Magdalen College, Cambridge.

Battle of Britain Memorial Flight – The museum is home to a collection of World War II aircraft including Spitfires, a Hurricane, a Dakota and one of only two flying Lancaster bombers. A flight plan board, by a small viewing area, shows daily take-off and landing times for aircraft going on ceremonial or display flights. The Flight is especially busy during the summer. (NB: the museum is only open for guided tours etc on weekdays. Tel: 01526-344041.)

Coningsby Church – Famous for the huge, 16 feet diameter, clock on the tower. Brightly painted, it is the largest one-handed clock in Britain (possibly in the world). External arches allow you to walk under the tower but outside the church.

REFRESHMENTS:
The Fortescue Arms, Tattershall.
The Black Horse, Tattershall.
There are also numerous possibilities in Coningsby.

Walk 17   SOUTH THORESBY AND HAUGH   3m (5km)

Maps: OS Sheets Landranger 122; Pathfinder 767.

A short, easy walk suitable for families of all ages.

Start: At 402768, the T-junction near the Vine Inn, South Thoresby.

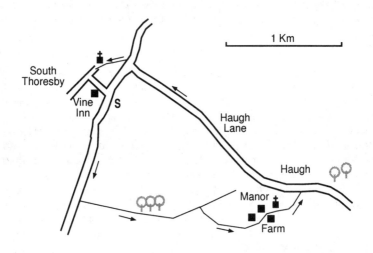

South Thoresby has narrow lanes and you may need to drive a little way towards Driby to find roadside parking. Parking is possible at the Vine Inn, but permission must be sought first and consideration exercised in leaving your vehicle.

From the T-junction, walk south-westwards, along the Driby road, for something over $^3/_4$ miles, then take a bridleway on the left. Go uphill along a field edge, pass a small wood, and continue beside a hedge. The way soon begins to veer leftwards downhill, and a footpath signpost is reached directing you to the right, across a field. The path is normally clearly marked through any crops, but initially you should aim for the house to the right of the farm buildings at Haugh. When you reach a farm road, turn left. Go over a cattle grid into the farmyard and bear right over a second grid by a fence. At the end of the fence you can double back to visit **Haugh Church**.

There is no right of way to the public road from here, but the owner of Haugh Manor has agreed to the use of the access road. Stay on this until the public road is reached.

Turn left and, with the views to your right stretching over coastal marshes to the sea, follow this quiet road to a T-junction near **South Thoresby**. Cross the stile opposite and bear half-left across a meadow, heading towards the church. Go through the churchyard to reach a road. Walk ahead and then take the first turning left to return to the start.

POINTS OF INTEREST:

Haugh Church – This tiny church is only about 50 feet long. It has a pretty ogee doorway and inside there is a Norman arch to the chancel. The church is largely constructed of chalk, looking its best on a bright day when the stone reflects the sunlight.

South Thoresby – St Andrew's Church is 18th-century and has a Venetian east window and geometric stained glass. The Old Rectory nearby, with its patterned brickwork and turret, was designed by the famous Victorian architect S S Teulon.

REFRESHMENTS:

The Vine Inn, South Thoresby.

Walk 18   MARSTON AND HOUGHAM   3³/₄m (6km)

Maps: OS Sheets Landranger 130; Pathfinder 814.

A short walk around two quiet villages in the Witham valley.

Start: At 892436, in School Lane, Marston.

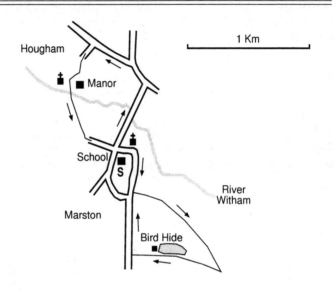

Marston is north-east of the A1 and some 4¹/₂ miles north of Grantham. There is not much parking space but School Lane provides some, if you keep clear of the school gates.

Walk back to the Thorold Arms on the corner of School Lane and Main Street, and turn right. Follow the road past the church and out of the village. Keep to the footpath, though it does change sides of the road about halfway, then take the side road to the left towards Hougham. Walk into the village and, near the green, turn left along Manor Lane. At its end, just inside the entrance to **Hougham Manor**, there is a footpath sign and, on the right, a kissing gate in a metal fence. Go through the gate and cross a paddock, heading to the right of a house, to reach another kissing gate (in another metal fence). Beyond this there is a bridge over the **River Witham**. However, before crossing it is worth visiting **Hougham Church** just to your right.

Once over the bridge, go left along a field path towards Marston. Cross a footbridge before joining Stonepit Lane on the edge of the village. (Note, on your way across the field, the traces of original brick paving and kerbstones for the path.) When you reach a road, turn left back into Marston village, crossing Main Street by the Thorold Arms to reach School Lane again. Now walk in the opposite direction, going past **Marston School**. At the corner near **Marston Hall**, turn right and continue along Barkston Road for about 300 yards, then turn left along a track signed as the Viking Way. When you reach two fieldgates close together, veer sharp right. At a track junction a sign for the **Bird Hide** indicates a very sharp right-hand turn. Walk to the bird hide and then continue to rejoin Barkston Road. Turn right back into Marston.

POINTS OF INTEREST:

Hougham Manor – There has been a manor house here since Norman times. Although most of the present building is of later date, a small amount of Norman work remains inside. The Manor stands on a charming moated site near the river.

River Witham – Here the river is some 18 miles from its source just over the Lincolnshire/Leicestershire border to the south-west. It has yet to flow north to Lincoln and south by Tattershall to Boston before turning east to enter the Wash. Here it flows due west.

Hougham Church – The church has a Norman nave and a Georgian chancel. Look for the engraved 'graffiti' from the 1800s on the south aisle windows. Amateur genealogists might like to try piecing together the Hickson family history: there are seventeen gravestones lined up side by side dating from 1830 to 1958. A particularly poignant small one at the end of the line is to 'P I H December 1899 to July 1900'.

Marston School – The school was built in 1861. Note the most unusual design: ornate brickwork with a fine tower and entrance set at a 45° angle to the main building.

Marston Hall – The seat of the Thorolds, a famous Lincolnshire family. The present Hall is of varying dates from the 16th century onwards, though the Thorolds have been here for 600 years. The present owner, the Rev H Thorold, is a well known writer on ecclesiastical architecture. The garden is renowned and occasionally opened to the public on summer weekends.

Bird Hide – East of Marston the river valley is low lying, the flooded area attracting many birds. A useful resting place-cum-picnic spot.

REFRESHMENTS:
The Thorold Arms, Marston.

Walk 19　HEMSWELL AND WILLOUGHTON　3³/₄m (6km)

Maps: OS Sheets Landranger 112; Pathfinder 729.

The lower slopes of the Lincoln 'cliff' provide a short walk between two charming villages.

Start: At 932908, Bunkers Hill at Hemswell.

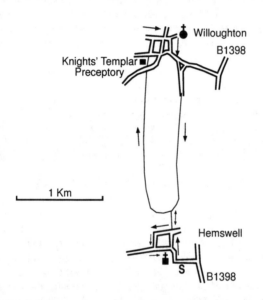

Hemswell lies north of Lincoln and east of Gainsborough, just off the B1398. There is little parking space in the village so the best place is on the descent of Bunkers Hill from the B1398 where obstruction can be avoided.

Walk down the hill and around to the right to enter Dawnhill Lane. At Brook Street, go half-right, by a telegraph pole, up a gravel drive between two houses. At a footpath sign, join a track which soon bends left, and then right near some trees. After about 1,000 yards, where the track bears right again, cross a footbridge on the left and go through a copse and over a fence. Continue forward beside the fence to its corner, then keep ahead over the field to reach a stile on the far side. Go over on to a road.

40

Cross the road to a footbridge and stile opposite. Beyond these, cross another field, aiming for a red brick house and noting the earthworks of **The Knights' Templar Preceptory**. Go through a white gate and along the lane opposite to reach a road junction. Turn right and walk into **Willoughton**. (Note the village post office/shop to your right, the inn is a few yards beyond it - but see refreshment notes.)

By the war memorial, cross into Church Street. Go through the churchyard, passing to the right of the church to reach a metal gate in the far wall and follow the short paved path beyond to a kissing gate. Go through and turn right, keeping to the right of a barn to reach another kissing gate. Go through, cross the road beyond and walk up Long Lane.

When the lane ends, keep forward along a grass path, which soon becomes more distinct, into a belt of trees. Continue until the trees end where there is a stile in a fence: go over and cross the field beyond, aiming slightly right to reach a stile by a red and white gate. Here you rejoin the outward route, follow it back in **Hemswell.** There, turn right down Brook Street, passing the Pinfold, and then walk up Maypole Street. Turn left to return to the start.

POINTS OF INTEREST:

Knights' Templar Preceptory – After The Crusades the Knights' Templar enjoyed special legal, religious and taxation privileges to assist in raising revenue for their cause. They had five Preceptories in Lincolnshire. These were as much administration as religious centres. Willoughton was the largest and wealthiest in England. No buildings remain, only earthworks and ditches now indicate the site, still known as Temple Garth, *garth* being an enclosed piece of land.

Willoughton – There were prehistoric settlers on the 'cliff' here and by Domesday it was known as *Wilchetone*. The church possesses a vamping horn, a rare, early type of loud hailer, used instead of bells to summon worshippers. Note the delightful old shop and Post Office, still displaying an ancient sign advertising savings bank, insurance and annuity services.

Hemswell–The brook from the springs on the hillside did indeed once run down Brook Street, but except in one or two gardens it is now covered. In Jubilee year (1977) the Pinfold, in which stray animals would have been impounded, was restored and given a bench seat. In that year, too, the huge maypole was refurbished. Its use on May Day has since been revived as an annual event.

REFRESHMENTS:

The Stirrup Inn, Willoughton. Lunchtime opening at weekends only.
Hemswell and Willoughton each have a shop.

Walk 20   SWABY AND SOUTH THORESBY   4m (6½km)

Maps: OS Sheets Landranger 122; Pathfinder 766 and 767.

A hidden valley, lakes, springs and a Nature Reserve.

Start: At 386771, Swaby church.

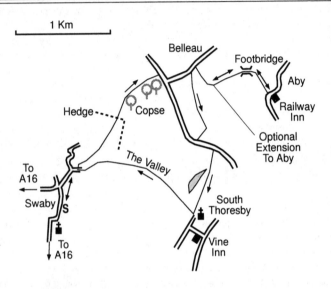

Swaby is 7 miles south of Louth. Parking is limited and the lanes narrow so do be considerate. Between Swaby and **Belleau** the route crosses open fields. These can be heavy going after rain.

Walk along Church Lane into the village, turning right at the crossroads into Pado Lane. At the first bend, turn right along a narrow lane and, after 50 yards, cross a stile on the left and go steeply uphill to the corner of a small wood. Now strike out across a large field, bearing slightly left, away from the valley seen below on the right. As you top the rise, head for a gap in the hedge 60 yards or so to the left of the field corner. After going through this the way is clearly seen. In the centre of the next field there is a copse: the path passes immediately to the left of this and continues across to the corner of the woods ahead. Walk along the side of the woods to reach a road. Turn right, and then, almost at once, left along a lane to Belleau.

(A very pleasant extension leaves Belleau just beyond the church. A farm track – by a brick dovecote – leads down past the Eau Springs and turns left along an instantaneous river. After two footbridges on the right, keep right to pass Aby's tin mortuary chapel to reach the Railway Inn. You must return the same way: there and back adds $1^1/_4$ miles.)

The walk continues along a footpath that leaves Belleau almost opposite the church gate, following a wire fence. Where this bends left, a signpost directs you across a field towards woods at the far side. Bear right at the woodland edge to reach a road and turn left. Cross Belleau Bridge and, at a signpost and stile on the right, cross into a paddock. Cross the paddock into a large grass field and continue, with a lake coming into view below and on the right. Aim to be about midway between the lake and the farm buildings up on your left: cross a stile in a wire fence and trend slightly left to reach a gate, stile and footpath signpost – with two fingers – near South Thoresby Church.

For refreshment, follow the lane beyond and take the first left. The Vine Inn is just up the hill.

The route goes sharp right back down the field, following the wall to a stile near a pond. The next field can be marshy but there is a sleeper causeway: head for the far right-hand corner to reach a footbridge. Cross and turn sharp left to enter a wooded valley. At a junction with a bridleway keep ahead, soon entering a **Nature Reserve**. Walk through this to a gate and go through into a beautiful garden with secret lakes. This is the right of way, but do stay on the footpath. Just beyond this idyllic spot you rejoin Pado Lane: reverse the outward route to the start.

POINTS OF INTEREST:

Belleau – An ancient settlement, going back to before Domesday. The site, with its vigorous springs, is typical of many along the fringes of the Wolds, where chalk meets marsh. The Tudor brickwork of the dovecote and parts of the old farm buildings are the only remains of the original manor.

Nature Reserve – The Reserve is managed by the Lincolnshire and South Humberside Trust for Nature Conservation. The valley, formed by glacial overflow, has a marshy bottom and chalk hillsides, each with its own typical flora and fauna. On the south of the stream are some further permissive footpaths opened by the landowner under the Countryside Commission Stewardship Scheme. Local information boards and maps are on display.

REFRESHMENTS:
The Vine Inn, South Thoresby.
The Railway Inn, Aby.

Walk 21 DENTON RESERVOIR AND GRANTHAM CANAL 4m (6¹/₂km)

Maps: OS Sheets Landranger 130; Pathfinder 835.

A short level walk including part of the canal towpath.

Start: At 866325, Denton Church.

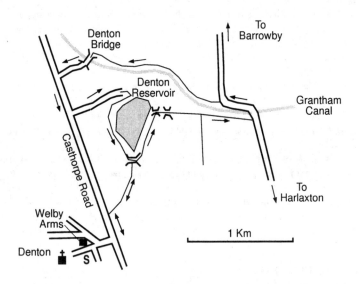

There is only limited parking available down the cul-de-sac by the church, so please park with consideration.

From the church, walk back to the road junction and continue to a T-junction. Turn left and walk out of the village to reach a signed footpath on the right, just after a bridge. Cross the stile and walk beside a stream, crossing further stiles and a track which was once a mineral railway. Just before reaching the reservoir, cross the footbridge on the right and turn left to walk around the reservoir edge. Follow the edge to reach a flight of steps on the right. Go down these to reach a footbridge, cross and follow a hedge to reach another footbridge and a stile.

Continue beside the hedge for a short distance, then veer left to reach a gap in the hedge ahead. Go through and keep forward, now walking high above the **canal**, on your left, to reach a stile and steps leading down to the road from Harlaxton. Turn left, cross the canal on the road bridge and descend to the towpath. Double back along the opposite bank for a mile to reach Denton Bridge, where there is a picnic site on the opposite bank. Turn left over the bridge and follow a track up to the road.

Turn left to reach, after about 300 yards, a track on the left. Follow this. The track eventually turns sharply to the right where a ramp leads up to the reservoir again: go to the right, following the reservoir bank to rejoin your outward route. Now retrace your steps back to the start.

POINTS OF INTEREST:

The Grantham Canal – The Grantham canal was built in 1793. It runs for 33 miles from the River Trent near Nottingham with a rise of 140 feet. It prospered until 1851 when the railway arrived in Grantham. After a few years, the railway company bought the canal, which finally closed in 1929. It is currently managed by the British Waterways Board and much restoration is taking place.

The reservoir was made as a feeder water supply for the canal. It has a capacity of over 60 million gallons and is a favourite haunt of anglers and many species of waterfowl.

REFRESHMENTS:
The Welby Arms, Denton.

Walks 22 & 23   ROPSLEY AND SAPPERTON   4m (6½km)
or 6m (9½km)

Map: OS Sheets Landranger 130; Pathfinders 835 and 836.
Old stone built villages, quiet lanes and a Roman road.
Start: At 994341, the southern end of Ropsley village.

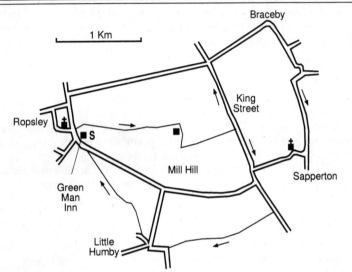

The road is wide enough to allow considerate parking. The last ½ mile back into Ropsley can be muddy after rain.

Walk back into **Ropsley**, passing the Green Man, and then take an uphill path on the right, near the entrance to 'Wuthering Heights', to join a farm track. Follow the track to some derelict farm buildings. Go sharp right immediately beyond these (a memorial seat gives an early opportunity for a break) and, after 200 yards, at a gate, go sharp left. Continue along the track and then a field headland to reach **King Street**, a green lane also called Long Hollow on OS maps.

The shorter route turns right here, following the lane to reach a road where the longer route is rejoined.

The longer route turns left, following the lane to reach a road. Go right, uphill, past the old village quarries, into **Braceby**. Walk through the village and, at the first

T-junction, keep straight on. At the second, turn right, following the road to **Sapperton**. Turn right to walk through the village. Beyond the church and Manor House, walk downhill past a pond and around a sharp left bend, rejoining the shorter route.

Go straight on at a T-junction and then take the first path on the right, after some electricity wires. Cross a footbridge and, keeping a hedge on your right, follow waymarkers over a series of stiles in an almost direct line to the road at **Little Humby**. Walk into the village and straight down past the green to reach the ford. Do not cross: instead, take the unmetalled lane a few yards to the right. After 150 yards, look for a footpath and stile on the right. Follow this path across two pasture fields and then, after crossing a stile and a footbridge, go left to reach a field corner. The next field is arable: go half-right to reach a stile near a large tree on the far side. Cross the next field to another stile, then cross a final field, bearing slightly right to round a small wood. In the field corner find a path that passes behind the gardens of several houses, finally emerging on a drive. Walk down this drive and turn left at the road to return to the start.

POINTS OF INTEREST:

Ropsley – A picturesque village and winner of 'Best kept village' awards. On a house in High Street (once the Peacock Inn) near the start a plaque commemorates the birthplace of Richard Fox in 1448. This 'local lad made good' was a leading churchman and statesman of his day, becoming Bishop of Exeter and later Bishop of Winchester. After Henry Tudor's victory at the Battle of Bosworth Fox became Secretary of State and Lord Privy Seal. He founded both the Grammar School in Grantham (where later Isaac Newton was educated) and Corpus Christi College in Oxford.

King Street – This Roman road forms an easterly loop from the Ermine Street, linking the Nene valley and Lincoln. Just north of Bourne it divides, the King Street branch heading for Ancaster, the other branch, known as Mareham Lane, going via Sleaford. Both are clearly traceable on modern maps, and considerable stretches are still used as motor roads.

Braceby, Sapperton, Little Humby – Each of these isolated villages, linked by quiet lanes, are built of the local stone and hidden away in the folds of the surrounding countryside. Two have medieval churches and all have old farms and manor houses dating from the 17th century or earlier. One at Braceby is dated 1653 and one at Little Humby 1631.

REFRESHMENTS:

The Green Man, Ropsley.
The Fox's Brush (named after the animal – not the Bishop) lies off the walk, on the road to Old Somerby.

Walk 24   DUNHOLME AND SCOTHERN   4m (6½km)

Maps: OS Sheets Landranger 121; Pathfinder 765.

This walk links, and explores, two attractive villages near Lincoln.

Start: At 025793, Dunholme Church.

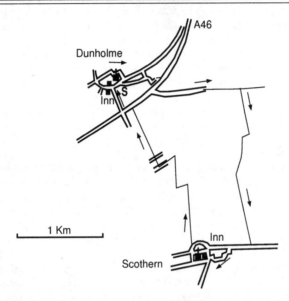

The two villages of Dunholme and Scothern are similar, both having their church, old houses and cottages clustered along the banks of a stream. There is an inn in each, so the walk could begin in either. Short tours in each are described. One field on the outward leg and the last two fields on the return to Dunholme are arable and could prove muddy at times.

Start facing **Dunholme** Church at the footbridge over the stream. Cross this, turn left and walk upstream until the ford is reached. Turn right and follow a lane around the back of the church to emerge at the churchyard corner near where you set off. The restored **Dunholme Spring** is in the wall to your left. Turn left and, after 250 yards, cross into Beck Lane. Beyond another ford, turn left at a junction and cross the bypass, with care, into a lane signed as a bridleway. Follow this around a left-hand bend and, after about 1,000 yards, take the headland footpath signposted on the right. In the field corner the path turns right for a few paces before crossing a stile and footbridge on the left. On the far side of the next field a track is clearly visible: this leads to the road near **Scothern**. Turn right towards the village centre. When you reach Craypool Lane, cross and follow it as it meanders to a junction with Sudbrooke Road. Turn right, and then left by the Glass and Bottle Inn.

The return route to Dunholme turns right into School Crescent. At the first corner a path goes ahead by a wall between houses. Bear right at a farmyard to join a track beside a playing field. Just after the track bends left, take a headland path on the right, at a waymarker by a hedge. At the field corner go left to cross two footbridges within 50 yards of each other, one on either side of a narrow arable field. From the second bridge, walk directly over a much larger arable field. If the path is not clear on the ground, aim first to converge with some telegraph wires at a double pole in the middle of the field, and then for a gap, which is left of centre, in a line of poplar trees ahead. You will reach the A46 again at a fieldgate: turn left, with care, and then right to return to Dunholme.

POINTS OF INTEREST:

Dunholme – Named *Duneham* in the Domesday Book when much of the land belonged to the sinister sounding Odo the Arblaster. St Chad's Church has a 14th-century leather satchel which was possibly used to hold the sacrament. The stream is the Dunholme Beck.

Dunholme Spring – This was bored out originally in 1892, to a depth of 100 feet, and has been recently restored.

Scothern – Flowing along Main Street is the Scothern Beck with lots of little bridges across to houses on its bank.

REFRESHMENTS:
The Lord Nelson, Dunholme.
The Bottle and Glass, Scothern.

Walks 25 & 26   HUGGATE AND HUGGATE HEADS   4m (6½km) or 9m (14½km)

Maps: OS Sheets Landranger 106; Pathfinder 666.

Above and through Wolds dales along ancient grass tracks.

Start: At 882554, the village road in Huggate, at the side of a farm.

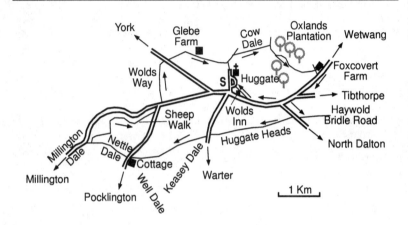

Parking is possible on the wider part of the village road. Please park considerately.

Walk towards the much narrower road, heading northwards and downhill, to meet the Wolds Way. Now keep right and shortly, a little uphill, cross the stile on the right, close to a gate. Descend Cow Dale to reach a path junction in front of Oxlands Plantation. Turn right over a stile and follow the track beyond along the edge of the plantation, following Oxlands Dale and then keeping slightly left along the bottom of Shortlands Dale with which it merges. The track rises and bears left: go through a gate and contiue to a T-junction. Turn right, go past Foxcovert Farm and then turn right at the road. Go past a junction on the left, continuing to reach a second junction.

The shorter walk continues ahead here, heading towards **Huggate**. Just before entering the village, turn right at a footpath sign and, soon, cross a stile on your left. Cross the unusual field beyond diagonally, avoiding a descent into the shallow chalk pits. Cross a stile and turn right, passing the village pond and St Mary's Church, to return to the start.

The longer route turns left at the junction to reach a bridleway which crosses the road. Turn right and follow this grass track along **Huggate Heads**. The track is part of the waymarked Minster Way: it crosses a road and passes above the heads of Keasey Dale and Well Dale. Cross the next road, by Cobdale Cottage, then go over a stile on the right to enter Nettle Dale. The path beyond is not clear, but goes close to a line of trees, sheep tracks through the grass making walking to the end of the dale easier. There the route meets the Wolds Way again, following it back to Huggate. Turn right, uphill, following a narrow track bearing right to reach sheep pens. Turn left at the end of the pens and go through a small wood. Exit the wood and turn right to go gently uphill, above **Millington Dale**, and along the old Huggate Sheepwalk. At the road, turn left to reach a road junction. Now go ahead, through a gate and follow a headland path to reach a track. Turn right, cross a road, and walk past the well-renovated Glebe Farm, steadily descending. At the junction reached on the outward journey, turn right and retrace your steps back into Huggate.

POINTS OF INTEREST:

Huggate – This lovely Wolds village occupies a sheltered spot on the side of a valley. It has a small village green and pond. St Mary's Church, its spire the only part visible from just a short distance to the west, was built, in the 15th century in Perpendicular style, on the site of its Norman predecessor. Farms abound in the village and its neighbourhood, with plenty of sheep to be found in the grassy dales.

Huggate Heads – This section of the old Haywold Bridle Road provides good views along a surprisingly level route to the south of the village. The Minster Way, part of which is followed by this route, joins Beverley and York Minsters.

Millington Dale – This beautiful dale is one of the most popular, its narrow road through giving easy access to Millington Pastures and Millington Wood, now a Nature Reserve. The lower part of the dale has wells and a stream, while most Wolds valleys are dry.

REFRESHMENTS:

The Wolds Inn, Huggate. This inn, on the Driffield road, is popular with walkers and cyclists.

There are also possibilities in both North Dalton and Millington.

Walks 27 & 28   **RAYWELL**   4m (6$\frac{1}{2}$km)
                                            or 6m (9$\frac{1}{2}$km)
Maps: OS Sheets Landranger 106; Pathfinder 686, 687 and 695.
Gently undulating country in the south-eastern Wolds.
Start: At 992306, Raywell House.

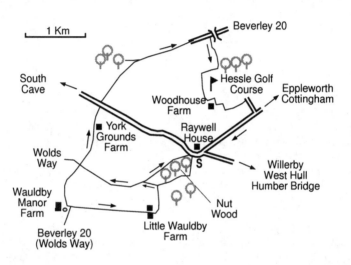

Parking is possible just off the roadside by Raywell House, but please park considerately.

Take the bridleway uphill to the left of **Nut Wood** and, at the top of the hill, turn right to enter the wood. Follow the narrow, winding path through the wood, keeping close to the bridleway which is now on your left. Rejoin the bridleway at the end of the path, then turn right, downhill, at a bridleway junction. Go left at the bottom of the hill, following a wide track up to reach the Wolds Way, where a bridleway crosses. This is part of the Beverley 20 waymarked route.

The shorter walk turns left here, through a gate, to reach **Wauldby Manor**. Turn left in front of the pond and continue uphill along the wide farm track, before gently descending to Little Wauldby Farm. Turn left at the T-junction and descend once again, following the route travelled earlier along the western side of Nut Wood. At the bottom of the hill, turn right to return to the start.

The longer route turns right, following a track uphill from the Wolds Way junction. After the climb, descend to reach York Grounds Farm and continue to the road from Raywell. Cross the road and continue along the bridleway a little to the left. Follow the bridleway along field headlands down into a valley at a bridleway junction. Turn right along a wide track. This diverts to the left at the end of the hedge and continues ahead. The track soon becomes wider. Now, shortly before reaching an old railway bridge ahead, leave the Beverley 20 route, turning right along a bridleway, going uphill with a hedge on your left. The bridleway follows field headlands upwards to reach a line of trees above **Hessle Golf Course**. The bridleway passes around the perimeter of the course as a narrow, enclosed track to reach the clubhouse. There, turn right down the access road and right again along Riplingham Road, passing Raywell Cottages to return to **Raywell House**.

POINTS OF INTEREST:

Raywell House – The House, a fine building, adjoins a large scout camp, further proof that this is a fine walking area.

Nut Wood – Now in the care of the Woodland Trust, this beautiful wood has masses of bluebells and garlic in the Spring.

Wauldby Manor – A fascinating group of buildings. You may have to walk a little round the pond to spot the small, now disused, church, and to get a good view of the Manor itself.

Hessle Golf Club – Despite the name, the course is nowhere near Hessle. It was established here when the original course was taken over for the building of the Humber Bridge.

REFRESHMENTS:

None en route, but those travelling back towards Hull, via the Humber Bridge approach road towards Willerby,will find two inns at the the first roundabout. Nearby is a McDonalds.

Walk 29   DANES DYKE AND SEWERBY   4m (6$\frac{1}{2}$km)

Maps: OS Sheets Landranger 101; Pathfinder 646.

Pleasant paths including woodland and clifftop walking. Some moderate climbs, one steep, but by-passable.

Start: At 215694, the car park at Danes Dyke, reached via the access road from the B1255. Free during the winter only.

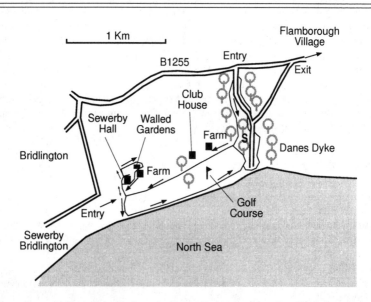

From the car park, walk back along the **Danes Dyke** access road and, at a short distance past the exit road junction, pick up the narrow nature trail path on the left. Follow the trail through a few trees close to the road before crossing to the right of the road and continuing along it as it rises steadily through woodland to the top of the valley. Close to the road entry, the path turns sharply and descends to recross the road, continuing below it, back along the valley. Eventually the path crosses the valley bottom and climbs to the top of the opposite side. Go past a path descending on the left which leads back to the start, and continue, soon reaching a footpath to Sewerby on the right. Take this path across the modern golf course.

Go through a gate and continue to the cricket pitch at Sewerby Park. Here you can either go directly to the cliff top or visit the Hall and grounds. There is a charge during summertime.

To continue the walk, turn right at the entrance and follow the path close to the left-hand side of **Sewerby Hall**, passing a small zoo, a café and a toilet block. Turn right along the path by the putting green and go through a pleasant garden area. Now cross a farm track and enter the walled garden ahead. Go through the exit at the far left-hand corner and walk through a second walled garden to reach an exit at its right-hand corner. The pleasant path beyond leads back to the entrance. Cross the farm track and keep left to pass along the left-hand side of the Hall. Turn along the front of the Hall, then retrace your steps to the cricket ground and continue to the cliff top.

Turn left to reach Danes Dyke. Take the path to the right at a junction, following it steadily down to the beach, with **Headland Way** signposts guiding you. Go straight up the steep steps at the opposite side. (These can be avoided by taking the easier track directly back to the car park.) At the top, turn left along the path above the valley, following it as it bears left and descends to a track. Turn right back to the car park.

POINTS OF INTEREST:

Danes Dyke – The area visited by this walk is a natural valley. This was extended during the Iron Age when a dyke was dug, and an embankment built, to reach the northern cliff top on Flamborough head. The valley is a lovely wildlife area.

Sewerby Hall – The Hall's grounds – very pleasant and well maintained. – include various attractions, while the Hall has much of interest, including a restored orangery and an 'Amy Johnson' room.

The Headland Way – This is the fourth and last of the series of 20 mile walks from the Humber Bridge to Filey, the East Riding Heritage Way. The Way starts at Bridlington Priory Church.

REFRESHMENTS:

There is a small kiosk at Danes Dyke during the summer and a café at Sewerby Park. There is also an inn at the southern end of Sewerby village, several in Flamborough and many more in Bridlington.

Walk 30   **MELBOURNE**   4m (6½km)

Maps: OS Sheets Landranger 106; Pathfinder 674.

A level walk along field and canal paths.

Start: At 753441, the Cross Keys Inn, Melbourne.

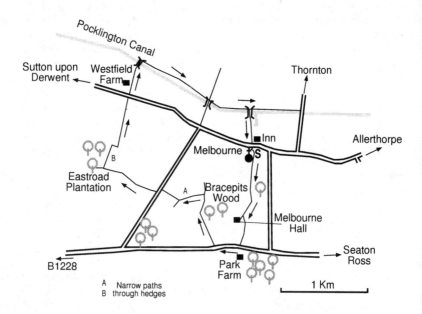

From the Inn, walk westwards to the telephone box. Cross the road and go down St Monica's Close, noting **St Monica's Church**. Now turn left along a concrete access road immediately after the first two bungalows. Turn right at the end, going along the path to the left of a brick building. Follow the path behind gardens to reach a stile. Cross this and the plank bridge beyond into a field.

Walk beside of a line of telegraph posts to reach a farm track and bear very slightly left towards a wooden fence. Cross and walk across a narrow paddock (controlling any dogs) to reach a stile. Go over on to a track and turn left. Soon, turn right at a junction, heading towards Melbourne Hall. Bear left and, when you reach a small open area opposite a grass track, cross the fence by the side of a gate into a narrow field. Beware of mud! Cross to the other side of the field and turn left to reach a gate in the far corner. Now bear right from your earlier direction, heading towards the right-hand side of Park Farm to reach a stile opposite the farm entrance. Cross on to a minor road and turn right.

Follow the road to just before a right-hand bend and turn right there along a wide track. Follow the track around the edge of Bracepits Wood, then keep to the headland on the right to reach the field corner. Leave the path and turn left along an unclear track, walking with a hedge on your right. Where the hedge bends left, take a narrow path, rather hidden by overgrowth, through the hedge. Cross a bridge over a drain to reach an enclosed **green lane** at a sharp bend and keep right to follow this, partially overgrown, lane to a road. Cross the road and walk a little to the left to reach a small, partly hidden plank bridge and stile.

Cross and bear a little left across a field, heading towards a fence corner. Maintain direction to reach a gap in the centre of the fence ahead, then bear a little to the right, heading towards the end of Eastfield Plantation. Follow the path into, and through, the plantation. Now go past a track from a field on the right, and, after a few more yards, turn right along a narrow track to reach an open field. Walk to its right-hand corner, go through the narrow gap in the hedge and cross a plank bridge and stile. Cross a footbridge on the right and turn left along the drain side to reach the field corner. There, cross a plank bridge just to the left of a tall tree, turn right and, soon, left at the corner to reach a track. Follow the track to the Melbourne road, passing Grove Cottage.

Cross the road and go along the access road to Westfield Farm. Keep ahead as this turns left, and cross the bridge over **Pocklington Canal**. Turn right along the grass towpath. Go past the first bridge reached and, later, cross the swing bridge. Now follow the track past a canal basin to return to the Cross Keys Inn at Melbourne.

POINTS OF INTEREST:

St Monica's Church – This modern church has an unusual small spire.
Green Lane – The lane's overgrowth includes gorse and numerous wild flowers.
Pocklington Canal – The canal is navigable to Melbourne. An assortment of boats may be seen in the basin.

REFRESHMENTS:
The Cross Keys Inn, Melbourne.

Walk 31   **AIRMYN**   4m (6¹/₂km)

Maps: OS Sheets Landranger 106; Pathfinder 694.
Easy walking along a riverbank and a quiet road.
Start: At 724251, on the road to the south-west of Airmyn.

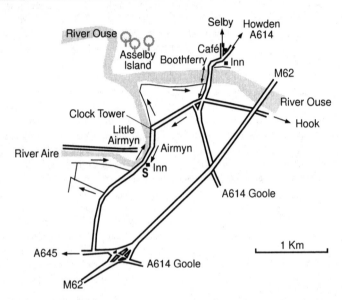

Take the road going south-westwards from **Airmyn** towards the A614. Just past the Airmyn village sign, turn right along a footpath by the side of a hedge, with a drain on your right. Follow the path to reach a footbridge over the drain and turn right to cross it. Follow the field-side path beyond, going straight ahead to reach the embankment of the River Aire. Turn right along the embankment, with the river on your left, and, beyond it, an interesting area of wetland. Airmyn is soon regained, but the route continues along the embankment, with the river now close by. Go past the lovely clock tower, continuing ahead to soon leave the village behind. There are a few stiles to cross along the way.

Continue to reach a group of trees and then descend from the newer and higher embankment to one a little lower, on the left. Follow this lower embankment to reach the confluence of the River Aire and the **River Ouse**. Now follow around, soon regaining the higher embankment, now with the River Ouse on your left. Continue to reach a narrow lane which goes a little way ahead, having come in from the right. Keep to the embankment, with a wall on your right, walking by the side of the lane. The lane is left behind as you approach **Boothferry Bridge**, with the modern M62 bridge not too far distant.

Pass under the older bridge and, immediately, climb up the narrow path to the right. Squeeze through a gap in the metal fence at the southern end of the bridge to reach the A164. Cross, with care, climb immediately over the low metal fence and go down to the river embankment, soon reaching a stile on the left. Cross and walk along the side of the car park of the Ferry Inn to regain the A164. If you wish, you can pause at the inn, or visit the Red Beck Café opposite.

Turn left, with care, crossing the road, with even greater care, just before reaching the bridge. Walk back to the southern bank and, soon, turn right along the quiet road back into Airmyn, keeping ahead at the crossroads. Go past the small school and either follow the road back to the start, or climb one of the flights of steps to return along the adjacent embankment.

POINTS OF INTEREST:

Airmyn – The village lines the bank of the River Aire, a pleasant embankment separating road from river. The clock tower merits a close look.

River Ouse – Water from a very wide area drains into the Ouse which joins the Trent at the start of the Humber Estuary. The river is used by small boats and, occasionally, larger ships.

Boothferry Bridge – For a long time this was the first river crossing point from the sea. It is still well used and occasionally opened for river traffic.

REFRESHMENTS:

The Percy Arms, Airmyn.

The Ferry Boat Inn, Boothferry Bridge.

The Red Beck transport café at Boothferry Bridge is also very good value.

Walks 32 & 33   TEALBY AND CLAXBY   4¹/₄m (6³/₄km)
or 8³/₄m (14km)

Maps: OS Sheets Landranger 113; Pathfinder 730.
A Lincolnshire classic: fine scenery and the 'Rambler's' church.
Start: At 156905, The King's Head car park.

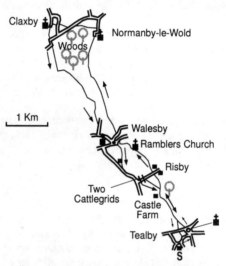

Tealby is a picturesque and popular village. Seek permission to park at the pub (and perhaps buy a pint later!) or park considerately elsewhere. Both walks are strenuous.

Walk uphill through Tealby (*see* Note to Walk 81), taking Front Street and Beck Hill. Go through the churchyard, turning left to join Rasen Road. After a few yards, take a footpath on the right by a white garage, veering left down the field. Cross a stile and walk uphill to another stile into woods near Castle Farm. Turn right to cross this and continue, crossing more stiles, until directed left at an access notice. Go downhill to a stile and gate (near telephone wires), and cross Risby Farm road. Go over another stile and cross a steep valley, climbing to the right of the woods on the far side. Cross two further fields on an obvious path to **All Saints' Church**. Go down the lane to a road.

The longer route leaves the shorter version here, rejoining it for the return to the start.

The longer route turns right, then left and right again along Otby Lane. After the house on the corner, take the path on the left and follow a headland towards a grey farmhouse, passing to its left. Cross a stream by footbridge to reach a bridlegate. Walk uphill to a second bridlegate, going left through it and continuing uphill over the wold top to **Normanby-le-Wold**. About 100 yards beyond the church, go left along a signed field path to a stile in a wire fence: a steep drop follows to a road near Claxby. Turn left for 200 yards, then right along a signed footpath and almost immediately left along another. A series of stiles indicate an obvious route over paddocks and a garden to a road. Take the path directly opposite, bearing left at a lane to reach **Claxby Church**. Beyond the church, follow a permissive path, then keep forward along a road. At a corner go ahead along a farm track to reach a fenced paddock. Turn left to a track junction and then bear right to continue to a junction with the Viking Way. Bear right by a hedge to join another track leading to the road at Walesby. Turn left, then right along a path to **St Mary's Church**. Turn left and walk to within a few steps of your outward route from the 'old' church, rejoining the shorter route.

Take the signed path by a new house, crossing a paddock behind it to reach a stile. Cross and veer right, passing behind another house to reach a stile on to a road. Go left to the Risby access road and turn left over the cattle grid. Cross a second cattle grid, then bear right, uphill, to rejoin the outward route. Retrace your steps but, at the outskirts of Tealby, keep to the right to reach a stile by a barn wall. Cross Rasen Road and walk down a field, bearing left to a final stile. The inn is to your right.

POINTS OF INTEREST:

All Saints' Church – All Saints' is the 'Rambler's' church with a stained glass window (1950) showing Christ with ramblers and cyclists. A ramblers' service is held every Trinity Sunday.

Normanby-le-Wold – 1,000 yards to the north is Lincolnshire's highest point at Normanby Wold Top at 168 metres (550 feet).

Claxby Church – The chancel arch carvings show grimacing faces, one with its tongue out, the other stretching its mouth open with its fingers.

St Mary's Church – The Reverend Percival Laurence (Rector 1879-1913) campaigned for 30 years for this church to replace the 'old' one, and died the day work began on 6th June 1913. It is most unusual because the nave is divided centrally by pillars and arches rising to the roof ridge.

REFRESHMENTS:

The King's Head, Tealby.

There is also a tea room in Front Street.

Walk 34   HUBBARDS HILLS AND RAITHBY   4¼m (6¾km)

Maps: OS Sheets Landranger 122; Pathfinder 748.

The wooded gorge of Hubbards Hills, a local beauty spot.

Start: At 321872, the junction of Love Lane and Westgate.

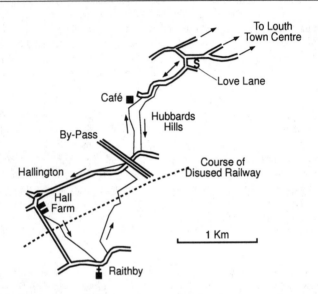

There is limited parking in Love Lane, but **Louth** has several car parks. If you park in town, walk past the church and along Westgate to reach Love Lane. There is seasonal parking at the café in Hubbards Hills. If you park there return along the road to the path by the wall.

Go through the gate in the white fence and cross Westgate Fields to reach a road. Turn right and after a left-hand bend, take a rising path to the left by a wall. The path climbs steadily above the valley, giving elevated views of the River Lud.

When the path descends, turn right down steps and then go left to reach a road. Turn right and walk under the by-pass bridge, then immediately turn right up steps into a field. Go left and walk parallel to the minor road for 400 yards to reach a footpath sign and a gate. Maintain direction along the road, bearing left at two junctions to reach a third (Withcall Lane). Just past this, on the left, a signpost points across Home Farm orchard. Cross the stile and head diagonally through the orchard. Cross another stile into the pasture beyond and go down to a third stile in the far left-hand corner. Climb over on to the old **Louth and Lincoln Railway**.

(Note – if the arable field ahead is likely to be muddy because of rain you could join the lane a few yards to your right to reach Raithby, or even stay on it from Hallington.)

Following the line indicated by the fingerpost, walk across the large field ahead until **Raithby** church comes into view. Now aim for it, crossing a stile in the hedge ahead. Cross the grass field beyond, going to the left of some houses to reach the road opposite the church.

Turn left along the road for 200 yards, then go left along a track that goes across the front of a joinery workshop. A path soon slants off to the right: take this, it is easy to follow, passing a lake, then going left over the old railway again and through woods. Now walk towards the by-pass, turning left to reach the road and then right under the by-pass again to return to Hubbards Hills. This time, walk along the valley floor, passing close to the café en route. Finally, retrace your steps to either Love Lane or the town centre.

POINTS OF INTEREST:

Louth – This has been a busy market town since Norman times, its main claim to fame being the magnificent parish church of St James. The spire is the highest of any parish church in the country, reaching 295 feet (almost 90 metres). It cost £305 in the early 1500s when it was added to the tower built some 70 years earlier.

The Louth and Lincoln Railway – This is crossed twice on the walk. Opened in 1876, it was bought out by the Great Northern in 1883. Passenger traffic ceased in 1951, freight carrying on until 1956.

Raithby – The 14th-century appearance of the church belies its 1839 rebuilding, although some of the interior is genuinely medieval. It stands in a most picturesque setting with a stream and its own pond in the churchyard. Note the old village pump near the gate as you join the road.

REFRESHMENTS:

The Wheatsheaf Inn, Westgate, Louth, is only a short distance from the start of the walk. The café in Hubbards Hills, is passed towards the end of the walk.

Walk 35   **Thorpe-on-the-Hill**   4¹/₄m (6³/₄km)
Maps: OS Sheets Landranger 121; Pathfinder 781.
Easy, level walking through a Nature Reserve and woods.
Start: At 911659, in Littleborough Lane, Thorpe-on-the-Hill.

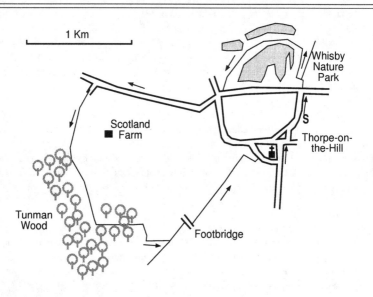

Thorpe-on-the-Hill is south-west of Lincoln and north of the A46. Parking space is limited so use the wide verges in Littleborough Lane, north of the village.

Walk north to a T-junction and take the footpath opposite for a few steps, then go through a green metal kissing-gate on the left into the **Redland Nature Conservation Area**. Bear right along the first wide lakeside path. Do not go through a second **green gate** on your right: instead, keep walking anti-clockwise round the lake. Half-way around, ignore a track going off to the right, then, after 3 'sides' of the lake, about 1,000 yards of walking, and where the path bears sharply left near a notice board, turn right to reach a road.

Turn right to reach a crossroads. Go straight on and, after another 1,000 yards, near a farm and a footpath sign on the right, take the unsigned track by the telegraph poles on the left. Follow the track to, and along the edge of, **Tunman Wood**. Keep ahead, following the waymarkers, when the track veers right into the wood. You can now see Lincoln cathedral to your left. At a waymarker where more woodland (Stocking Wood) stretches away to your left, turn left. At its far end, turn right and walk to a field corner. Turn left beside a hedge, soon joining another path. Turn left again and, after 200 yards, cross the footbridge on your right, resuming your original direction to join a farm track at the field corner. Walk on towards Thorpe-on-the-Hill.

Now, before some farm buildings, take the fieldpath over a stile on the right, crossing a grass field to another stile in the far left corner. At the road turn right. Beyond the church, turn left into Fosse Lane, passing the **John Hunt Memorial Chapel**. Turn right at a junction: the first left is Littleborough Lane.

POINTS OF INTEREST:

Thorpe-on-the-Hill – This has been a settlement since at least Norman times. In the Domesday Book it was known as *Torp* but by 1281 had become *Torp-sur-le-Tetre*. The 'hill' is 87 feet high.

Redland Nature Conservation Area – To the south-west of Lincoln there has been extensive working of glacial gravels leaving many such pits as this. Here the Redland Gravel Company is re-landscaping their old workings and many varieties of water fowl have moved in, including cormorants.

Green Gate – A second gate at the north-east corner of the lake gives access to Whisby Pits, a further 51 acres of Nature Reserve managed by The Lincolnshire and Humberside Trust for Nature Conservation. A detour during, or a visit after, the walk would provide extra interest, especially for bird watchers.

Tunman Wood – Woodland since the 1770s, the wood was privately owned at first but is now managed by the Forestry Commission. North Kesteven District Council publish a leaflet of waymarked walks in the surrounding area.

John Hunt Memorial Chapel – This was built in 1909 and commemorates a ploughman who lived locally in the early 1800s. He educated himself, became a missionary and went to Fiji where he died at the age of 36, having translated the Bible into Fijian.

REFRESHMENTS:

There are none on the walk but just south of Thorpe-on-the-Hill at the junction of Fosse Lane and the A46 is *The Highwayman Inn*. There is a Little Chef restaurant next door.

Walk 36   STOKE ROCHFORD $4\frac{1}{4}$m ($6\frac{3}{4}$km)

Maps: OS Sheets Landranger 130; Pathfinder 855.

Tranquillity, leafy lanes, lakes and streams: all within a stone's throw of the A1.

Start: At 924273, where the Stoke Rochford lane leaves the A1.

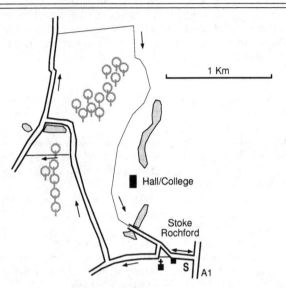

Parents may bribe their children on to this walk with the promise of a 'Big Mac'. 'McDonalds' is 200 yards up the A1 from the start. And with a footpath all the way you can even walk there too! An area of disused ground by the Stoke Rochford turn provides parking. There is also a small space near the Hall entrance, and just round the corner from the church. The directions start from the A1.

Walk away from the A1 and take the footpath on the left just after the shop/Post Office. Go down the field to a footbridge over a stream, cross and walk uphill to reach a kissing gate. Go through into the churchyard at **Stoke Rochford**. Walk through and, at the road, keep ahead to pass the village pump. Walk uphill and take the first turn on the right - a private road only to vehicular traffic. Ignore the first turn to the left to walk past a disused factory.

Opposite the next house, take the signed bridleway on the left, following it up a field to a bridlegate giving access to woodland. Continue forward – if anything, going fractionally left – to emerge at a gap in a fence. The woods stretch away to your right and ahead to your left: keep forward, first by the woods and then by a hedge, to reach a road. Turn right and follow the road to a T-junction just beyond the lakes of Home Farm.

Continue ahead along the road to reach a footpath on the right by a black barn. Take this and, at a junction of tracks, turn right again. Go left at some woods and, almost immediately, go right at a signpost and gate on to a golf course. Head for a group of trees to the left of a small wooden shelter, then continue to another group of trees by the 13th tee – there are waymarkers – where you join a metalled track. Turn right along the track, with views over a lake, until you pass the front of **Stoke Rochford Hall**. Walk down the Hall's drive and go over the bridge by another lake to reach the entrance gates and the road. Keep ahead to return to the start.

POINTS OF INTEREST:

Stoke Rochford – Two areas of parkland surround the village, to the north and south. These have been the ancestral homes of the Turnor and Cholmeley families respectively. The church has chapels for the monuments of each. These north and south chapels also reflect the geography of the families homes: Turnors to the north, Cholmeley to the south. In the churchyard, note some unusual metal headstones looking like gearwheels from ancient machinery. Look, too, for the ornate village pump.

Stoke Rochford Hall – It is known that the Romans occupied this site. The present Hall was built in the 1840s, an earlier one being down near the lake at the entrance. Part of the old stable block still stands by the drive. The obelisk opposite the house was erected in honour of Sir Isaac Newton, born 2 miles to the south at Woolsthorpe. The Hall is now a training centre of the National Union of Teachers.

REFRESHMENTS:

There are none on the walk. There is a 'McDonalds' roadhouse 200 yards north from the start on the A1 and a shop in Stoke Rochford.

Inns can be found in the neighbouring villages of Ponton, Colsterworth and Skillington, all within 5 minutes drive.

Walk 37   HOLBEACH MARSH $4^1/_2$m ($7^1/_4$km)

Maps: OS Sheets Landranger 131; Pathfinder 837 and 838.

For birdwatchers and aircraft spotters. Solitude, with views across the Wash.

Start: At 408338, at the end of a narrow lane.

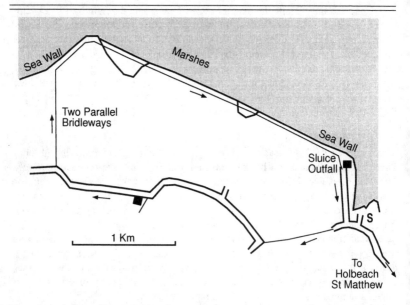

There is a telephone box at Grid Reference 411325: drive down the 'No Through Road' next to it until a parking area is reached along a potholed turning on the right.

This route is well waymarked. The marshes can be dangerous. Please heed the warning signs.

    Walk back to the lane where the tarmac ends and turn right. Go straight on at a metal gate, following a grassy track past some nesting boxes on poles and a pond, eventually joining a stony farm road. Follow the road when it becomes a concrete road. When it veers left you will reach an old concrete wartime bunker: bear right here and, when the road bears right, keep forward on grass again to reach two bridleway signs close together.

Turn right at the second sign and walk along the bank top to reach the newest outer sea bank. (There are two more bridleway signs.) Turn right and follow the top of the bank. As it bends right extensive views across The Wash and **Holbeach Marsh** are revealed.

Continue along the sea bank until a large sluice outfall is reached. (The bank loops inland by lagoons to your right at a couple of places. You can detour along these if you wish.) Cross the sluice and then turn right, following either the bank or the track below it to return to the start.

POINTS OF INTEREST:

Holbeach Marsh – Take binoculars with you on this walk – there is much to see. The area typifies the Fens with their magnificent skyscapes. On the marshes and lagoons there is a wide variety of birdlife, whilst, practising aerobatics of another kind, RAF jets swoop and dive over their targets out in the Wash. To the north-west Boston Stump church can be seen.

The approach to the start of the walk is over twisting lanes crossing rich black farmland. Holbeach itself, now well inland, was a small port in the Middle Ages - such is the change wrought by land reclamation over the centuries. A vast parish exceeding 20,000 acres it stretches some 15 miles inland. Four outlying communities and their churches are dedicated to the four apostles; Matthew, Mark, Luke and John, though you won't find St Luke's on the map! This church is actually at Holbeach Hurn.

REFRESHMENTS:

None en route. There are possibilities in Holbeach and other inns nearby:
The Bull's Neck, Penny Hill.
The Saracen's Head, Saracen's Head.
The Ship Inn, Fosdyke Bridge.
There is also a transport café at Fosdyke Bridge.

Walk 38 BRINKHILL AND WARDEN HILL 4¹⁄₂m (7¹⁄₄km)

Maps: OS Sheets Landranger 122; Pathfinder 766.

Superb views on a crossing of one of Lincolnshire's narrowest hill ridges.

Start: At 369734, a green lane with ample parking south-west of Brinkhill.

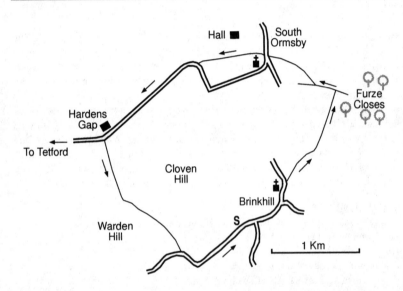

Brinkhill is west of the A16 and 10 miles south of Louth, in an area known as 'Tennyson Country'. The poet Alfred Lord Tennyson was born at nearby Somersby.

Walk into Brinkhill and turn left at the T-junction. Just beyond the church, take the signed footpath on the right, following it around an artificial lake on your right. Continue across fields to reach a T-junction with a farm track, about 100 yards out from Furze Closes Wood, to your right. Turn left along the track to reach a gate. Go through and bear half-right on rising ground. Cross two grass fields and pass behind a thatched cottage to reach the road at **South Ormsby**.

Cross into the churchyard and make for a small handgate in the far right-hand corner. Now walk ahead along a thin path across the park, through two five bar gates, on either side of a belt of trees – possibly the remains of an avenue approaching the house, and then ahead on a clearer path parallel to a grassy bank to reach a road beyond another gate. Go ahead, along the road to reach Hardens Gap Farm.

At the farm a footpath sign directs you up left: walk alongside a new fence and over the ridge of **Warden Hill**. On the descent, ignore the footpath on the right, continuing downhill to join the green lane which links Bag Enderby and **Brinkhill**. The start is at the end of this, turn left to reach it, ignoring another footpath signed to the right.

POINTS OF INTEREST:

South Ormsby – The village is dominated by the Hall, designed by Thomas Paine, and built between 1752 and 1755, with its park and lake. Viewed across the park St Leonard's Church looks most impressive. It has stonework spanning eight centuries. A Norman doorway (around the back of the tower) probably came from nearby Calceby Church where only ruins now remain. The stained glass in the Lady Chapel is reputed to have come from Paris' Notre Dame Cathedral during the French Revolution.

Warden Hill – One of Lincolnshire's narrowest hill ridges. There are superb views over Tennyson Country on either side.

Brinkhill – The church, built in 1857, has striking layers of alternate brick and local greenstone. There is a pottery in the village specialising in terracotta ware.

REFRESHMENTS:

The Massingberd Arms, South Ormsby. The inn is just off the route, about 500 yards north of the church.

There is nothing in Brinkhill, but there are other good local inns:

The White Hart, Tetford, to the west.

The George and Dragon, Hagworthingham, to the south.

Walk 39   **TENNYSON COUNTRY**   4¹/₂m (7¹/₄km)

Maps: OS Sheets Landranger 122; Pathfinder 766.

A walk to the birthplace of Alfred Lord Tennyson. Secluded countryside and marvellous views.

Start: At 334748, Tetford Church.

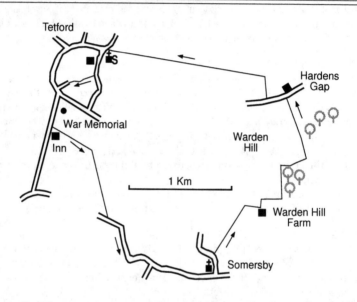

The road is wide enough for safe parking near the church, and the White Hart Inn is only a few yards away.

With your back to the church tower, turn left and walk down the road past the White Hart Inn. At the first bend, go right along a footpath, following it over a field to a footbridge. Cross and turn right along a lane, bearing left to reach a road. Turn left and then right by the War Memorial. Now take the track on the left, by the side of the Cross Keys Inn. The track soon narrows to a path and bends right to eventually reach a narrow lane. Turn left along this lane, following it for just over ¹/₂ mile to reach **Somersby**. On the way a small abandoned quarry on the left makes a sheltered picnic spot.

Turn left up the lane beyond Somersby Church and, after 200 yards, go right up a steep track to Warden Hill Farm. Keep to the track as it bends through the farmyard and then goes sharp left and very steeply down into, and then up out, of a hollow. Near the top, go right to reach a junction of paths by a fence. Turn left to continue the climb over the ridge of Warden Hill. Go straight down the other side to reach a road.

Turn left for 150 yards, then take a signed footpath on the right. The path goes along a headland for a short way before turning left and making a bee-line for Tetford - as it should, since it takes the line of a Roman road! The path crosses a series of stiles and footbridges, finally going over rough pasture to enter Tetford churchyard through a small gate. Walk through the churchyard to return to the start.

POINTS OF INTEREST:

Somersby – 'Tennyson Country' contains all that is best in the scenic attractions of the Wolds, an Area of Outstanding Natural Beauty. Somersby of course is a magnet drawing poetry lovers from far and wide.

The church dates from the early 15th century, and like many in the vicinity, is built of the local greenstone. Near the porch is a fine medieval churchyard cross. Inside is a fascinating display of Tennyson memorabilia.

Alfred Lord Tennyson was born on 6th August 1809 in the former rectory (now Somersby House – and not open to the public) which is just opposite the church. His father, George Clayton Tennyson, had come here in 1808. Alfred went to Louth Grammar School and a local printer published some of his earliest work in 1827. He became Poet Laureate in 1850. Much of his writing reflects his Lincolnshire childhood and the countryside in which he grew up. The famous 'brook' runs through the fields behind the house. He died on the 6th October 1892 and is buried at Poets' Corner in Westminster Abbey. His fathers tomb is by the church tower.

Near the church is Somersby Grange, a strikingly designed house built in 1722 and looking like a castle. Architectural historians consider that it may well have been designed by Sir John Vanbrugh, more famous as the architect of Blenheim Palace and Castle Howard.

REFRESHMENTS:

The White Hart, Tetford.

The Cross Keys, Salmonby.

A short drive away, at grid reference 358704, is Stockwith Mill (*Philips Farm* in Tennyson's poems) which has a craft centre and tea-rooms.

Walk 40   MORTON AND DYKE $4\frac{1}{2}$m ($7\frac{1}{4}$km)

Maps: OS Sheets Landranger 130; Pathfinder 856.

An easy ramble from a picturesque village on the fringe of the fens.

Start: At 098240, Morton village green.

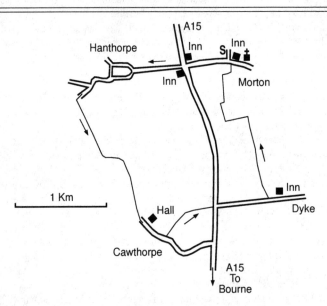

With your back to **Morton** church, walk up High Street and cross, with care, the main A15 road to continue along the road towards Hanthorpe. On nearing the village, bear right at a road junction and then, at the top of the village, bear left along The Grove. Now follow the Edenham road to reach, just beyond the last house, a track signed to Cawthorpe (and also as a Cycle Trail) on the left. Take this, following it as it bears left. Go straight on at a track junction near woodland to reach Cawthorpe.

Do not take the first footpath on the left: instead, continue forward, passing The Hall. Just beyond a pair of cottages, climb a stile on the left and walk up the small paddock beyond. Cross two stiles close together, go over a footbridge, and bear half-left across two fields (the path is usually well marked in any crops). Aim between the last two, on the left, of the row of trees ahead. Cross another stile and footbridge, and turn half-right to walk beside a hedge, following it to reach the A15 again. Cross, again with care, and walk into **Dyke**: the Wishing Well Inn can soon be seen ahead.

To continue, take the footpath on the left near house No. 5. At the end of the garden there is a signpost: go half-left across a field to reach the signpost visible on the far side. There, turn half-right, go past a post with a waymarker, cross a footbridge and keep straight on over the next field, bearing left along a grass track at the other side. When you reach a footpath sign, go over a sleeper bridge, cross a stile and go right to walk between a wire fence and an ancient hedge. Cross a stile on the right near a metal gate and, after 20 yards, cross another on the left. Head to the far right-hand corner of the field beyond to reach a (final) stile. The path beyond crosses the Vicarage drive and then goes left down another gravel drive to emerge near the church.

POINTS OF INTEREST:
Morton – The large cruciform church dominates the green. The porch, with an ancient nailed door, is set into the base of the tower and unusually faces to the west, so that it looks over the green and the High Street. The village has many old, attractive houses and cottages. The Grange has an almost château-like appearance with two conical lodges guarding the entrance. Look for the beautiful Venetian windows of the vicarage (seen towards the end of the walk) and the humorous crossed cleaver emblem over the butcher's shop.
Dyke – Seen from the walk is the only remaining smock mill in Lincolnshire.

REFRESHMENTS:
The Five Bells, Morton.
The Kings Head, Morton.
The Lord Nelson, Morton.
The Wishing Well, Dyke.

Walk 41   WITHAM-ON-THE-HILL   4½m (7¼km)

Maps: OS Sheets Landranger 130; Pathfinder 877.

A gentle walk, in rolling countryside, from a beautiful stone village.

Start: At 055163, the Six Bells Inn, Witham-on-the-Hill.

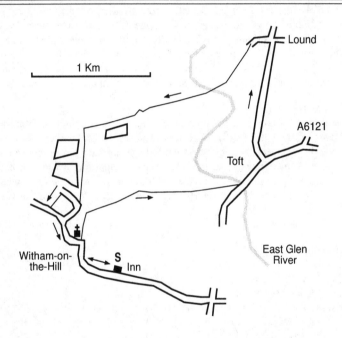

Parking is with the landlord's permission: please use the rear car park.

From the inn, turn right and walk through the village to the church. There, turn right just beyond the churchyard, going through a kissing gate and walking straight down the field beyond. At the bottom, cross two stiles and a footbridge over a stream. Now walk uphill between a hedge and a wire fence and then turn right along a gravel track. The gravel track becomes a dirt track, and then a grass track going slightly left at a waymarker to reach a three-way signpost.

Continue ahead, through a hedge and, at a field corner, go through another hedge. Cross the field beyond, going between two telegraph poles, but nearer to the right-hand one, aiming for a grey-roofed house. At a hedge gap there is another waymarker: continue heading for the house to reach the main A6121 road.

Turn left and, with care, walk into Toft, by-passing the bridge by using the ford and stepping stones below it on the left. After the hotel, take the lane on the left signed to Edenham. After about 1,000 yards, at a crossroads and a footpath sign, turn left along a lane. Follow the lane, which becomes unsurfaced at a compound fenced with concrete posts and wire, to reach a bridge. Cross and bear right, uphill, on field headlands, heading towards woods near Witham. Eventually waymarkers direct you through the hedge on your right, then left on the opposite side. At another waymarker, bear right by the woods to reach a farm road. Turn left back to Witham.

At the surfaced road – by Mill House – turn right for 200 yards, then take a signed footpath on the left, just before a track, and by a wooden panelled fence. Follow the footpath up to the main road. Turn left and walk back through **Witham-on-the-Hill**, admiring the stocks and the lovely old buildings.

POINTS OF INTEREST:

Witham-on-the-Hill – This is an exceedingly attractive village, with a 'Best Kept Village' award, and one with a long and varied history. St Andrew's Church is unusual in having its tower offset to the south where normally a transept would be. Nearby on the corner of the green are the village stocks.

The nearby Victorian school, built in 1847, has a 'straight to the point' motto carved upon it, which many might consider just as appropriate today!

Palace Farm, on the corner east of the church, is so named because it was once (though then it was much larger) a palace of the Bishops of Lincoln. King John is reputed to have stayed there in 1216 not long before he died.

The Hall was long a home to the Johnson family, one of whom, Archdeacon Johnson, was founder of the famous schools at Oakham and Uppingham. It is now a preparatory school itself.

Walkers may wonder at the location of the Six Bells on the extreme edge of the village. Early this century the inn was just opposite the Hall gates, but the local squire became exasperated at continually losing his grooms to the inn stables. His solution was to move it!

REFRESHMENTS:
The Six Bell, Witham-on-the-Hill.
The Toft House Hotel, Toft.

Walk 42 HAVERHOLME AND THE SLEAFORD CANAL $4^1/_2$m ($7^1/_4$km)

Maps: OS Sheets Landranger 130; Pathfinder 815.

The area around the Sleaford canal is full of natural and historic interest.

Start: At 106496, the car park at Haverholme Bridge.

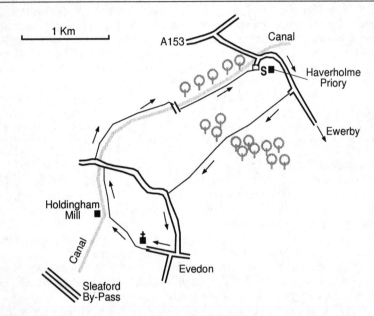

Haverholme is north-east of Sleaford, just off the A153. The walk starts with a short section on a road, albeit a quiet one. Nevertheless take care with children and pets.

Leave the car park and turn right. After passing farm buildings, **Haverholme Priory** comes into view on the right. Turn right along a track by a bridge opposite a lodge and follow this through woods to reach a lane. Turn left for **Evedon**.

Turn right in the village and right again along a 'No Through Road'. Pass the water tower and Manor House, taking the track on the right after the church. Walk downhill to ford the Old River Slea (there is a footbridge) and follow the grass track beyond to join the **Sleaford Canal**. The buildings opposite are the remains of **Holdingham Mill**.

78

Turn right and walk beside the canal to reach a road near the site of **Evedon Paper Mill**. Cross both road and canal to continue, with the canal now on your right. After about 1,000 yards there is a permissive path through a garden to a track over a bridge.

On this final stretch all semblance of walking by a canal is lost as you progress through overhanging trees towards Haverholme Lock. You may continue on either bank back to the start.

POINTS OF INTEREST:

Haverholme Priory – A Gilbertine priory was founded here in 1139 (*see* Note on St Gilbert in the Points of Interest to Walk 2). The present ruins are all that remain of a house built in 1830 and partly demolished in the 1920s, though it retained the 'Priory' name.

Evedon – A village has been here since before Domesday. The Manor House and church are the oldest buildings. The impressive brick water tower, now a most unusual house, was built in 1915. The church has an unusually low tower which is developing a list because of subsidence. Near the porch are rare examples of graves with horizontal stone lids.

Sleaford Canal – Constructed to connect Sleaford and the River Witham in 1794, this canal, like many others had a short life, being effectively deprived of trade by the railways. It closed in 1878. Now looking more like a river it is home to many species of water birds.

Holdingham Mill – The canal waters were also harnessed to operate several mills. Here one old mill partially survives and some of the water-wheel can still be seen. In the house garden is a small octagonal hut once used by the toll collector.

Evedon Paper Mill – No buildings remain here but if you cross the footbridge the overgrown mill-race is discernible. The nearby lane, part of which was walked earlier up to Evedon village, is still called Papermill Lane.

REFRESHMENTS:

None on the walk, but the *Finch Hatton Arms*, Ewerby is 3 miles away to the east. There are also possibilities in both Sleaford and Heckington.

Walk 43   CAISTOR AND NETTLETON   4¹/₂m (7¹/₄km)

Maps: OS Sheets Landranger 113; Pathfinder 719.

A Roman town, the surrounding hills, and part of the Viking Way.

Start: At 119013, Caistor Market Place.

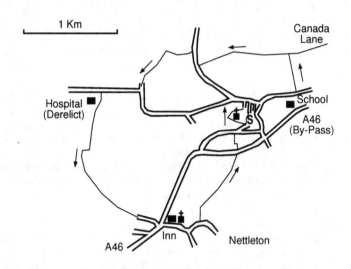

Park in the Market Place, behind the War Memorial by the White Hart Inn, or off High Street, behind the Town Hall.

Go into Cornhill, at the upper left-hand corner of the Market Place and walk through to High Street. Turn right up Grimsby Road. Beyond Spa Top take the footpath on the left across the **Water Hills** to Canada Lane. Turn left downhill to Brigg Road and turn right. After 100 yards, cross to a footpath by a caravan site sign. Follow the path over three stiles to a grass field, then continue ahead beside a stream to another stile on the left. Cross this and a footbridge, and climb steps on the other side. Shortly, at a waymarker, bear half-right to a lane which leads to Kelsey Road. Turn right and, after 400 yards, take a narrow path on the left just after Eirene Farm. Skirt the grounds of a hospital to reach open fields, where a raised grass path leads straight ahead. At a signpost, turn right for 20 yards, then go left (no waymarker) along a headland to a stile in the field corner. Cross and turn left, between trees, to a stile and metal gate. Cross a footbridge over a stream and bear left behind a small brick building. Re-cross the stream, then bear slightly right towards a house to reach a stile in the field corner. Follow the lane beyond to the A46 and cross, with care, to the Salutation Inn.

Walk into **Nettleton**. Beyond the church, turn left up Mansgate Hill. On the left at the first bend is a sign 'Footpath to Caistor'. This is the Viking Way. Keep to the right of a bungalow and, from the field corner, follow an obvious waymarked path, with stiles, across fields towards Caistor and a concrete ramp up the bypass embankment. Descend another ramp on the opposite side where a fenced path skirts a playing field and gardens. At the road turn right, and right again to reach some lock-up garages: take the path on their left to Nettleton Road. Cross, turn right, and then bear left below the school into the Horsemarket. To your right is the **Pigeon Spring**. You could return to the start up Plough Hill, but to see more of **Caistor** turn left into **Fountain Street** to see the **Syfer Spring**. Beyond, go up the steps into the churchyard. Keep ahead at first, then bear right around the church to the **Grammar School**. Walk up Church Street and Bank Street to return to the Market Place.

POINTS OF INTEREST:

Water Hills – From the top there are spectacular views. As you descend Canada Lane the source of some of Caistor's springs can be seen in the valley.

Nettleton – The ironstone tower to the church is exceedingly weathered and has a buttress which almost entirely conceals a tiny window.

Pigeon Spring – This is a small walled basin by the roadside. The fire engine was once kept in a tunnel behind the nearby doors set into the hillside.

Caistor – The Romans had a walled encampment here. As you walk along the southern edge of the churchyard you are above a section of Roman wall. The church is a mix of styles, but part of the tower is Saxon. In 1681 much of the town was destroyed by fire.

Fountain Street – Unusually the road nameplate also bears the former name of *Duck Street*.

Syfer Spring – Another of Caistor's ever-flowing springs. This one has never failed, even in the severest drought.

Grammar School – This was founded in 1630 with a bequest in the will of Francis Rawlinson, a local clergyman, born in 1564 at Market Rasen.

REFRESHMENTS:

The Salutation Inn, Nettleton.
There are numerous opportunities in Caistor.

Walk 44   **WOODHALL SPA** $4^{3}/_{4}$m ($7^{1}/_{2}$km)

Maps: OS Sheets Landranger 122; Pathfinder 782.

A gentle walk from this attractive spa town to a ruined abbey,
returning through woodland.

Start: At 194632, the car park in the Broadway, Woodhall Spar.

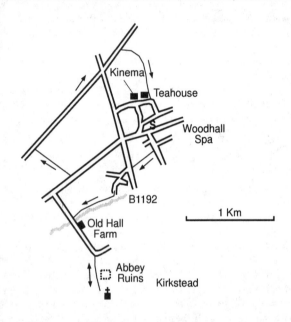

The car park is opposite the Eagle Lodge Hotel, and on what was once the railway line
to Horncastle.

From the car park entrance, cross the road and turn left. Walk along the Broadway, then
take the first turn right along Stanhope Road. Opposite the junction with Iddesleigh
Road, turn right again into Long Avenue, an unsurfaced footpath with no street name
plate at this end. On reaching Tattershall Road, turn left for a few paces, then cross into
St Leonard's Avenue. Bear left into St Leonard's Close, walk past a cul-de-sac and,
beyond the last house, take a footpath on the right. Follow the path alongside a stream

(shown on large scale maps as 'The Sewer' – an allusion to its origins perhaps!) to reach a road. Turn left and walk to a sharp left-hand bend. Here, walk ahead along a track to reach the site of **Kirkstead Abbey**. Continue past the ruins to **St Leonard's Church**.

Return to the road and walk back the way you came. Notice the remains of the abbey fishponds in the fields to your right: the Old Hall, on your left, was built with stone from the abbey ruins. Continue along the road to reach a T-junction. Turn right, then after about 200 yards, take the footpath on the left, part of the Viking Way. Follow the path across fields to reach another road. Turn right and walk to a crossroads.

Go straight over and continue for a further 300 yards to the end of some woods. Turn right on to a track along the wood edge, soon bearing half-right along a wide grass avenue, with trees on either side. The avenue soon narrows down to a footpath which joins a road beside The Teahouse in the Woods. Turn right across the front of this, pass the old spa buildings and the quaint **Kinema in the Woods**, veering left into Coronation Road. The next turn left, King George Avenue, leads you back to the start in the centre of **Woodhall Spa**.

POINTS OF INTEREST:

Kirkstead Abbey – This Cistercian abbey was founded in 1139. The impressive tower was part of the south transept. The other buildings have now gone, but grassy mounds give an indication of the abbey's extent.

St Leonard's Church – This delightful small church is renowned as a rare survivor of 13th-century architecture. Built about 1230, it was spared at the Dissolution (because it was outside the abbey gates) and fell into disuse in the 1880s. It was restored in 1914.

The Kinema in the Woods – Built as a concert pavilion in the heyday of Woodhall as a spa, it became a cinema in 1922 and still flourishes. It operates a unique back projection system and maintains its 1920s decor. During intervals an organist rises from the 'pits' to entertain.

Woodhall Spa – Now known for antiques, golf and as a retirement place, Woodhall Spa had unlikely beginnings. In 1821 a local entrepreneur, John Parkinson, convinced that he would find coal, started borings and discovered underground springs instead. The waters were rich in iodine and bromine but the spa was slow to develop, even after the railway arrived. It did eventually become a very popular place in Edwardian times. The 'coal mine' is commemorated on an elaborate town sign seen as you travel in from Stixwould to the north. The spa closed in the 1980s.

REFRESHMENTS:
There are numerous possibilities in Woodhall Spa.

Walk 45   OSBOURNBY AND THE TALLY HO INN   5m (8km)

Maps: OS Sheets Landranger 130; Pathfinder 836.

Attractive stone villages and views from a hilltop ridge.

Start: At 069381, near Osbournby church.

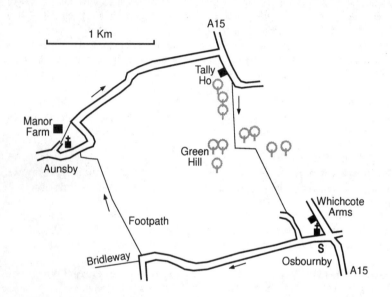

There is ample parking space in the village centre or by the church.

Walk into the wide Market Place. Take the lane leading westwards out of the village from the far left corner, following it for almost a mile until it bends sharply left. A bridleway continues ahead here, but our route takes the footpath which angles off up the field to the right.

   Aim for the pylon just to the right of **Aunsby** church spire, only the tip of which is visible. Although you do not gain much height there are extensive views in both directions on this section of the walk. Cross a ditch by a footbridge and continue across grass towards Aunsby. At a waymarked gate, go left and cross a small field diagonally to reach a second gate. Now go right to reach the road.

Turn left and walk as far as the church. Now double back sharply down the lane behind it. At the entrance to Manor Farm, climb the stile in the fence on the right and cross the grass field beyond, keeping right of the farm buildings, to reach a road. Continue along this quiet road for about a mile to its junction with the A15. There follows a short stretch on this road which can be busy, so take special care for the next 300 yards. Turn right, passing the Tally Ho Inn. Beyond the gate near a left-hand bend, turn right at a footpath sign.

After crossing a ditch by a footbridge, keep right again, heading towards some woods. In the field corner, turn left and walk uphill, keeping to the edge of the field, against the woodland. Eventually you will go up a broad grassy slope ahead: before the fence at the top a narrow path goes left into more trees and then contours along the hillside for a 100 yards or so. Where the trees end, find a ruined handgate in the fence on the right and admire the **view** before going a little further uphill to reach an equally fine view down the other side of the ridge.

Go straight down by the hedge to join a lane leading back into **Osbournby**, following it back to the Market Place.

POINTS OF INTEREST:

Aunsby – A small and very secluded village. Parts of the church date from Norman times and those walkers with very keen eyesight, or with binoculars in their rucksack, may be able to make out the 'Ave Maria' carved around the finial of the spire.

View – The view takes in the parkland of Aswarby Hall, seat of the Whichcote family, the local landowners, and its estate village. George Bass, the explorer who mapped much of South Australia with Matthew Flinders (from nearby Donington) was born in the village in 1771.

Osbournby – Iron age coins have been found in the area, so this is an ancient settlement. Shown in Domesday book as 'Osberneby', it has never been a large village, reaching a population of about 650 in the mid-19th century and currently being about a third of that. The spacious village centre, surprising for such a small village, was originally a proper green and years ago was the scene of a major event in the village calendar, the 'Osbournby Feast' with side shows and roundabouts. It was certainly established by 1783 and continued into this century. It now survives as a village fete.

REFRESHMENTS:
The Tally Ho Inn, Aswarby.
The Whichcote Arms, Osbournby.

Walk 46   **DUNSTON AND WASPS NEST**   5m (8km)
Maps: OS Sheets Landranger 121; Pathfinder 782.
Woodland, Fen and a Roman canal.
Start: At 063629, Dunston Church.

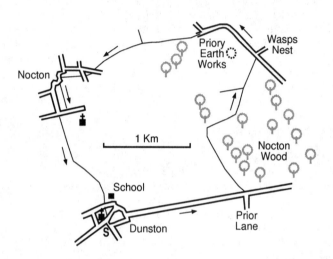

From the church, turn into Chapel Street and then go left into Front Street. After the bend, bear right across the green by the river, then go over a footbridge and walk along the road out of the village. After a mile, opposite Prior Lane, turn left up a track by Nocton Wood. Follow the track to reach a signpost on the right, by a gap in the trees. Turn right and walk along a track towards a plantation of silver birch trees. At a gate, go diagonally left across a grass field to reach a green metal gate. Turn right and walk down a stony track to the houses and road at **Wasps Nest**.

Turn left and follow the road round a left-hand bend. Now, where the road bends right, go ahead along a farm track. When this bends to the right, keep ahead along a grass path, with a stream on your left, to reach a stile. Cross and bear left over grass, with groups of houses on either side. Cross two roads to reach a stile in a wire fence. Cross and go towards more houses, slightly to the right, and then walk through a small copse to reach a road. Go left and walk around a left-hand bend. Now, where the road bends right, by the entrance to **Nocton Hall**, walk forwards down a drive by some houses. The drive becomes a path leading through to the school. Turn left here if you wish to visit the church.

The route turns right to reach the main road and then goes left down a lane almost opposite the Post Office. This lane leads directly back to **Dunston**. Near the school, turn right for a few paces, and then go left on another path through to Middle Street. Turn right to return to the church.

POINTS OF INTEREST:

Wasps Nest – This isolated farming hamlet on the edge of the fens was named after an inn that was planned, but never built. The walk goes around two sides of Abbey Hill. Earthworks are all that now remains of an Augustinian Priory established here in 1135.

Nocton Hall – Nocton has one of the most lavish Victorian churches in Lincolnshire. It was designed by the famous architect Sir George Gilbert Scott, who had a busy time in the village: he also designed the school and a row of cottages near the Hall's entrance. An earlier Hall burnt down in 1834 and was replaced in 1841. It has latterly been an RAF hospital.

Dunston – On Dunston Heath, 3 miles away (at grid reference 509619) is Dunston Pillar, built in 1751 by Sir Francis Dashwood as an aid to travellers. It was in effect an inland lighthouse with its lantern well over 100 feet high. Before the enclosures the Heath was a desolate place where it was easy to get lost, and travellers were at the mercy of highwaymen.

REFRESHMENTS:

The Red Lion, Dunston.
Other good local inns are:
The Chequers, Potterhanworth, $2^1/_2$ miles to the north of Dunston.
The Star and Garter, Metheringham, $1^1/_4$ miles to the south of Dunston.
The White Hart, Metheringham.
The Lincolnshire Poacher, Metheringham.

Walk 47   **BLANKNEY AND SCOPWICK**   5m (8km)

Maps: OS Sheets Landranger 121; Pathfinder 782 and 798.

An easy walk on lanes and fieldpaths between two charming villages.

Start: At 075606, the car park for walkers on the edge of Blankney village.

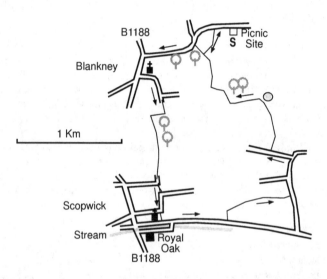

Paths in this area are maintained to a high standard by the North Kesteven District Council, with attractive parking areas and picnic sites provided. Well waymarked, they are easy to follow. However, some have been re-routed and the walk instructions do not always correspond with paths shown on the maps. The villages rival those of the Cotswolds, especially Scopwick, with its wide stream and a lane on either side, overlooked by the inn and old houses.

Walk through the picnic area at the end of the car park and cross two stiles, turning left along a grassy track beside a fence. At a stile in the fence, turn right, away from it, going through woods to reach a road. Turn left through the village of Blankney to reach a

T-junction with the B1188. Turn left for 200 yards, then, beyond the green by the church, take the metalled lane to the left. The lane bends round to pass Hall Gardens. At a left bend, go ahead along a farm track that bends right, then left to round some woods. When the lane bends right again, go straight ahead on grass to reach a handgate. Go through on to a wide green lane. Now, at the corner near some bungalows, take the path ahead between them to reach Scopwick church.

Turn right to reach the B1188, cross to the other side of the stream, and walk back along the other side – Brookside. Cross the stream again at any convenient point (there are several bridges) and walk out of the village. Just beyond the last new house, take the signed footpath on the left. This passes a paddock and then veers right to reach a metalled lane. Turn left along the lane, then take the second waymarked track on the left. Shortly, turn right and, beyond a gate, walk with a hedge on your right. Veer left by an overgrown pond to join a farm track, and then go slightly left at a waymarker, keeping a shallow, but deepening, ditch on your left. Bear right to reach some woods and, part way through them, turn left. After about 60 yards, go right and then continue forward to reach a waymarker by a concrete bridge over a dyke. Cross this and a stile and go straight across a pasture to reach a stile in the fence near the start. Cross to return to the car park.

POINTS OF INTEREST:
The primary interest on this walk is the villages themselves with their charming stone houses and cottages. The great events of history seem to have passed them by. At Blankney, in particular, the ornate stone work is worth seeing. The Hall burnt down in 1945, but the surrounding parkland and trees are delightful. Scopwick's picturesque setting is created by its stream. Both villages have attractive, though not especially noteworthy, churches.

REFRESHMENTS:
The Royal Oak, Scopwick.
There is a picnic site at the starting point, in Blankney.

TETFORD AND RUCKLAND 5m (8km)
or $8^1/_2$m ($13^1/_2$km)

Maps: OS Sheets Landranger 122; Pathfinder 766.
A walk over scenic hills and valleys of the Wolds.
Start: At 333780, in the short lane leading to Ruckland church.

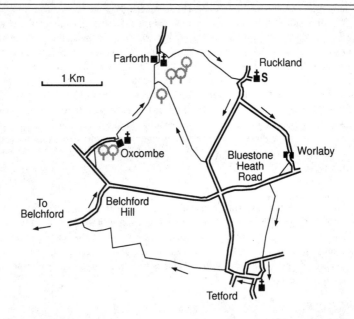

Set off on the road down the steep **Ruckland** hill to reach a track on the left leading to Worlaby.

The shorter route goes straight on here, following the road uphill for about 1,000 yards. Where the road bends left near a plantation, take the track on the right. Follow this downhill to the corner of a wood. Here a waymarker on the left directs you into the woods and along a steep downhill path. At the bottom, cross a stream and turn left for a short distance to join the path between Oxcombe and Farforth. The longer route is rejoined here, though a detour left up to **Oxcombe** is worthwhile, returning the same way.

The longer walk takes the Worlaby track. Beyond cottages, the track bends right, then left and right again, skirting the farm. Look for a stile on the right and cross the small pasture beyond to reach the Bluestone Heath Road. Turn right for 200 yards, then take a track on the left. Turn off this at a fingerpost high on the right bank, crossing two fields to reach a group of trees on the hilltop. Now descend towards Tetford. Keep well left of a copse in the middle of the field and aim for a cottage with a red pantiled roof and the church beyond. Go through the cottage garden and follow the lane opposite to the church. The White Hart Inn is to your left. Take the road opposite the church gate. Ignore a lane coming in from the right and, at the next junction, keep right. At a sharp right bend walk forward along a farm track. After 500 yards this divides: keep left and continue to reach a white footbridge. Cross, turn right and follow the waymarkers through alternate left and right turns to reach the road below Belchford Hill. Go right, uphill, to rejoin the Bluestone Heath Road. Turn left, but after 350 yards, take the field path signed on the right. Aim diagonally left to the corner of some woods to reach a lane. Turn right to Oxcombe, making a detour through the farm to see the church. Those taking the detour from the shorter route rejoin here. The shorter route itself is joined closer to Farforth.

Take the track opposite the letterbox in the house wall, following it as it bears right down a valley and heads for Farforth. Continue to Farforth, turning right through the farmyard. Turn left up the lane and then take the track on the right immediately beyond the church. At a gate, leave the track, keeping trees and a stream on your right. This path leads directly back to Ruckland.

POINTS OF INTEREST:

Ruckland – The church has a Nordic appearance and is dedicated to St Olave, a Norwegian prince. He fought against the Danes in England in 1014, returned to Norway as king in 1016 and died in battle in 1030. There has been a church here since Norman times. The present one was built in 1885.

Oxcombe – This is a remote church not visible from the road. Indeed, not seen until you have passed through the farmyard of Oxcombe Manor. The church was built in 1842 (though there was a church here for centuries before that). Its octagonal tower, pinnacles and many interesting features are described in a guide, but for most people its charm lies in its quite unexpected location and the sense of discovery that one has in finding it.

REFRESHMENTS:
The White Hart, Tetford.

Walk 50   **WELL VALE AND ULCEBY**   5m (8km)

Maps: OS Sheets Landranger 122; Pathfinder 767.

Farm and woodland tracks, and the beautiful parkland of the
Well Vale estate.

Start: At 442737, on the road near Well.

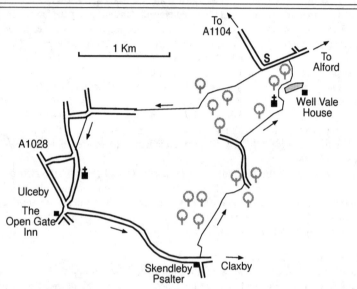

Park on a wide grass verge at the sharp bend near Well. Please do not obstruct nearby gates.

Climb the stile at the road corner and walk through the woods. At the far side a signpost and stile on the right point to a field path, a well-defined grass strip. Follow this path towards **Ulceby**. When it joins a farm track, keep forward, ignoring a side track to the left, to reach a waymarked T-junction of tracks near the farm. Turn left, and almost immediately right as if to enter the farmyard, but instead of doing this bear left to reach another waymarker and stile in a fence a few feet away. Be careful, the stile may be concealed by machinery. Go over the stile and diagonally across the pasture beyond to the far right-hand corner, reaching a road near a pond and phone box. Go left along the road, walk uphill past the church in Ulceby.

At a road junction, turn left along the minor road signed to 'Claxby'. This quiet road gradually descends a charming valley for a mile to Skendleby Psalter. Opposite the farm, go left along a signed footpath. Walk up the track, around the back of a house, and then continue uphill beside some woods. Eventually the path bears right by a hedge to reach another signpost. This directs you to the left along a track inside some more woods. In a few yards, where the track divides, keep to the left, and at the next track junction go sharp right. Now walk along the edge of a large grass field with woods to your left to reach **Well Vale** Church from which the valley, with its house and lake, is suddenly and impressively revealed.

Turn sharp left across the front of the church and steeply descend the hillside before bearing right to round the end of the lake. Walk above the lake to reach the corner of some woodland and then turn sharp left to reach a final stile. Cross this on to the road and turn left to return to the start.

POINTS OF INTEREST:

Ulceby – Ulceby Grange Farm has an unusual castellated silo, looking like a church tower from a distance. The quaint red brick Church of All Saints was built in 1826 and restored in 1885. It has a beautiful hillside site, shaded by large trees.

Well Vale – An unusually beautiful landscaped parkland, the church having a dramatic view between its massive Tuscan style columns down to the house. This was entirely intentional of course as it was deliberately aligned to the front door. Inside are inward facing pews, a gallery and Royal Arms. A 1916 Lincolnshire guide book (J C Cox) made quite derogatory comments about it. How tastes change! The house was built in 1725 and the church in 1733.

REFRESHMENTS:

The Open Gate Inn, Ulceby.
There are also possibilities in Alford only 5 minutes drive northwards from the starting point.

Maps: OS Sheets Landranger 122; Pathfinder 748.

A delightful village and lake, and marvellous views from high open wolds and country lanes.

Start: At 322834, the crossroads north of Tathwell.

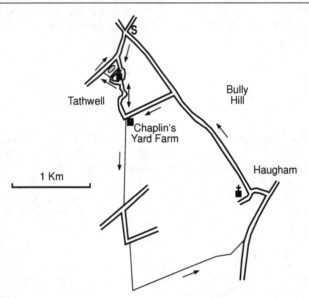

Tathwell is just over a mile to the west of the A16, some 2 miles south of Louth. Parking in the village is limited so please use the verges near the crossroads.

Walk down into Tathwell and turn left before the lake along a lane which gradually winds uphill out of the village. Ignore the first right turn and a right turn near the Old Post Office, continuing to a farm called Chaplin's Yard, where the lane bends left.

    Take the signposted bridleway which goes uphill and slightly to the right. At a hedge, keep forward, walking with the hedge to your right. When the hedge ends, go over an arable field aiming for the left-most gap of several in the hedge on the other side, and aiming well left of a clump of trees in the middle of the field. Cross a second field in the same direction to reach a track running along its far side. Another track leaves this to continue in your direction of travel: walk along it until it bends left, then keep ahead along a grass path. The path drops into a hollow where there is a waymarker on a post. After a short rise it dips into a smaller hollow from where a grass track goes off to the left: follow this for 1 mile to reach a road.

Turn left, and left again at the first road junction. Follow the road (with a short diversion to the left at **Haugham** to see the church) for nearly $1^1/_4$ miles, then, at the next road junction, a left turn brings you back to Chaplin's Yard. Reverse the outward route back to Tathwell, but at the Old Post Office corner walk ahead along a tree-lined grass path to reach the church. Turn left by the porch and go down steps to reach a lane by the lake. Go into a drive opposite, but only for a few paces, and then bear right past the end of the lake. The path leads over a hill to reach a road. Turn right back to the start.

POINTS OF INTEREST:

Tathwell – This is a secluded place, tucked away in a quiet valley. The church is largely 18th-century, built of brick upon an earlier stone base. It is dedicated to St Vedast, a 6th-century French bishop. Inside is a 17th-century monument to the Hanby family. Edward Hanby was Lord Mayor of London in 1626.

On Bully Hill, passed on the return to Tathwell, there are prehistoric burial mounds.

Haugham – Those who have travelled via Louth may think that they are seeing things here. The church, built in 1837 by the vicar, the Rev. G Chaplin, at his own expense, was deliberately designed as a miniature of the magnificent St James' in nearby Louth. It is now maintained by the Redundant Churches Fund.

REFRESHMENTS:

None en route, but there are plenty of facilities in nearby Louth. The nearest country pubs are:
The Royal Oak, Little Cawthorpe, 3 miles to the east.
The Stags Head, Burwell on the A16 3 miles south-east.

Maps: OS Sheets Landranger 121 and 122; Pathfinder 747.
The western foothills of the Wolds provide both solitude and great views.
Start: At 183844, the Heneage Arms in Hainton.

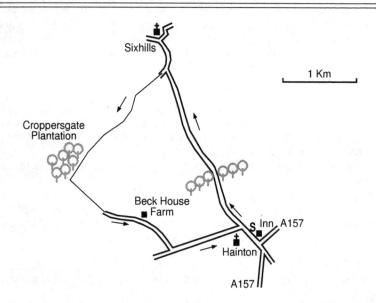

Hainton is on the A157 between Louth and Wragby. Turn off and find parking on the Sixhills road. About half the walk is on country roads, but these are very quiet and have good views, east to the higher Wolds and west to the Witham valley with Lincoln Cathedral clearly visible on the skyline. One short stretch of bridleway near Croppersgate Plantation (GR 159854) can be rough and muddy underfoot.

Walk along the Sixhills road, passing the school, (and noting the large outside bell in its bell-cote) for about 1¼ miles to reach, at a right-hand bend, a bridleway going off to the left.

At this point it is worth proceeding the extra short distance to the pretty hamlet of **Sixhills** and its church. Return to this spot.

The bridleway is fairly level for the first 1,000 yards, then narrows and dips down between hedges to reach a metal gate. Go through this and continue downhill beside a high hedge for 200 yards to reach a marshy area with a pond on the left. Now veer slightly left over rough pasture, keeping to the right of a large clump of gorse. This grassland attracts a variety of butterflies in summer. Aim for the left-hand corner of some woods (Croppersgate Plantation), going through another metal gate to join a track alongside them.

At a junction with a farm road, turn left, following the road until it becomes a metalled lane. After about a mile, at a T-junction, turn left back to **Hainton**.

POINTS OF INTEREST:

Sixhills – The small Victorian church was built in 1869. Inside is a beautiful wooden ceiling of unusual scissor-beam construction. Outside there is wrought ironwork on the chancel roof and a gravestone near the porch carved to look like a tree trunk.

Hainton – The Heneage family have lived in the Hall since the 14th century and a family chapel in the church is full of monuments. The church was rebuilt in 1848 by architect Edward J Willson, though the obviously new spire dates from 1974, the work following a lightning strike. Willson had a long working association with the Heneage family during the 1830s and 1840s, virtually remodelling the whole village. The hall, the stables, the school, the inn and various houses and cottages are all his designs. There is a framed history of his achievements in the church porch and his tomb is a few yards away, under the trees.

REFRESHMENTS:

The Heneage Arms, Hainton.

There is also a small village stores/Post Office on the minor road, signed to Torrington, passed on the walk.

Walk 53   BEVERLEY AND THE WESTWOOD   5m (8km)

Maps: OS Sheets Landranger 107; Pathfinder 687 and 676.

Mainly grassland walking on the Westwood, with good views around, and a fascinating walk through the streets of Beverley.

Start: At 041392, the well signposted Army Transport Museum on Flemingate (the Hull road) in Beverley.

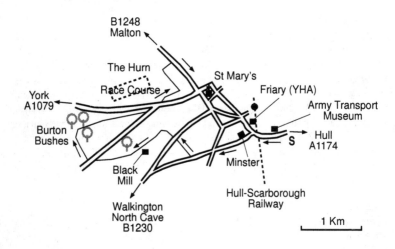

From the start in **Beverley**, walk towards the nearby Minster, cross the road and continue along its southern side. Straight ahead is Keldgate, where an old hospital, with a coat of arms on its wall, is quickly passed. Cross the A164, with care, and take the Walkington road to reach the **Westwood**. Tracks of short grass cross the rougher areas: turn half-right along a wider track heading towards the tops of bushes, crossing a minor road to reach Newbegin Pits. Take the left side and, at the corner, turn left along a track to reach Black Mill. There, bear right towards the left-hand side of a group of bushes and go down into the small valley. At the boundary fence, turn right alongside it, following it across a road to reach the entrance to **Burton Bushes**. Go through a gate and follow the wide track beyond to reach another wide track on the right. Turn down this, ignoring crossing tracks, to reach a stile. Go over to return to the Westwood. If conditions in the wood are very muddy, you may prefer to keep to the first track, which also returns to the Westwood.

Follow tracks south of the racecourse grandstand, generally heading towards the distant St Mary's Church, to the left of the Minster, and going gently downhill to reach the road junction below. Cross to an information notice board alongside Newbegin Pits, and then cross the A1079, with care. Turn right, alongside the racecourse (which is on Hurn Common), and then turn left alongside house gardens. A short stretch of narrow concrete path now leads to a gate on to Gallows Lane.

Turn right, down the lane, and go right again at the bottom, soon passing the Law Courts. Cross over at a junction and go through North Bar. Pass alongside St Mary's church and go left immediately down Hengate. Soon, turn right along Ladygate which, after crossing Sow Hill, emerges at the southern end of Saturday Market. Bear right, and then left, down the pedestrianised Toll Gavel and then bear left along Butchers Lane to reach the Wednesday Market. Now take the Hull road (Eastgate), but just before reaching the Minster, turn left, through metal gates, to go along Friary Walk. At the Friary (YHA), bear right, between walls, and go through a brick gateway. Cross the footbridge over the railway, pausing to get a good view of the Friary, then turn right to reach the main road. Now retrace your steps to the museum.

POINTS OF INTEREST:

Beverley – A lovely historic town. A guidebook is needed to describe all its delights adequately, but all visitors will see much to fascinate them. Gems include the beautiful St Mary's Church and the magnificent Minster. The Army Transport Museum can easily occupy several hours of time.

Westwood – The Westwood is one of five local Commons. The walk also visits the Hurn. The Westwood is very popular for walking, horse riding, and golfing. The route crosses a golf course: take care, but remember that you have the right to walk anywhere on the Common. The Newbegin Pits area is popular with children.

Burton Bushes – This woodland dates back about 1000 years and is now enclosed to protect it from the cattle which roam freely on the common.

REFRESHMENTS:
There is ample opportunity in Beverley.

Walk 54 TOPHILL LOW WATERS 5m (8km)

Maps: OS Sheets Landranger 107: Pathfinder 676.

Very flat walking along grass banks of a river and drain, both rich in wildfowl. Dogs may cause friction near Nature Reserve.

Start: At 061471, Wilfholme Landing.

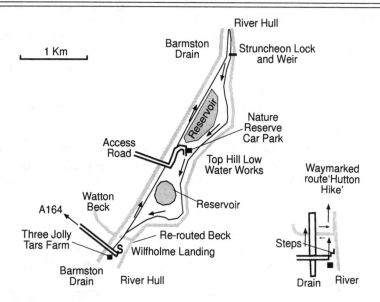

The start, near the River Hull, is reached along the minor road that heads eastwards from the A164, to south of Watton.

Go up steps and through a small gate to reach the bank of the River Hull, just to the north of the Three Jolly Tars Farm at **Wilfholme Landing**. Turn left along the riverbank, with Barmston Drain on your left. The course of Watton Beck has been altered and, to cross it, you must follow the path to the left and go through a gate. Now turn right, cross the beck, and immediately right again to regain the river. Continue beside the river until it bends right and drop down there to reach the bridleway which follows the bank of Barmston Drain.

The bridleway passes a man-made pond, on the opposite bank, and widens just before reaching the access road into **Top Hill Low Water Works**. This is also the access to the **Nature Reserve**.

Continue ahead (unless you wish to visit the Reserve first), following the path, which remains on the drain side. As it passes a large reservoir, a concrete road runs beside it. Before long, woodland is reached on your right and a bridge on the left gives access to a path alongside the old course of the River Hull. Do not take this path: instead, keep to the drain's bank until a gate is reached. Go through to regain the bank of the river and turn right to reach **Struncheon Lock**.

As you walk along the meandering river bank, you will pass woodland and swampy areas and ponds: walk quietly as this is part of the Nature Reserve and disturbance to the wildfowl should be kept to a minimum.

Eventually, you will reach the point where earlier you left the riverbank. Now retrace your steps to the start at Wilfholme.

POINTS OF INTEREST:

Wilfholme Landing – Small boats are moored on the river here. The Three Jolly Tars Farm was an inn when barges used to ply regularly between Hull and Driffield.

Top Hill Low Water Works – The works supplies the city of Hull. Yorkshire Water have helped to establish the **Nature Reserve**, which is open from 9am to sunset on winter weekends and daily during the summer.

Struncheon Lock – Now restored, the lock is where the River Hull becomes tidal. Water is extracted just up the river, the water cascading over the weir helping to make this a restful picnic stop.

REFRESHMENTS:

None available en route. Hutton Cranswick, a little to the north along the A164, has three inns along its main street and Beverley and Driffield, each with cafés and plenty of inns, are both relatively close.

Walk 55   **NORTH CAVE AND HOTHAM**   5m (8km)

Maps: OS Sheets Landranger 106; Pathfinder 686.

Easy walking through two old villages and pleasant countryside,
including Hotham Hall grounds.

Start: At 892323, Main Street, North Cave, near the White Hart
Inn and a chapel.

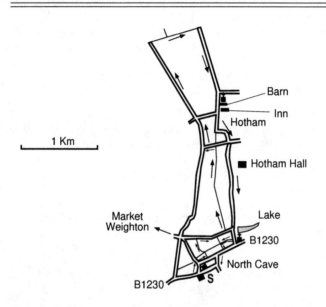

From almost opposite the chapel, walk down Blanshards Lane. Turn right along
Church Street and then turn left down Mill Lane. Soon, take the narrow footpath to the
right of the wide entry to the old mill. Cross the footbridge over the beck, noting the
mill race, and go through a kissing gate. Turn right along Nordham and cross the road
to reach a footpath on the left. The path is almost straight, going along the western side
of the grounds of Hotham Hall to reach a narrow road at Hotham. The walk can be
shortened here, either by turning right, or by using the footpath opposite to reach the
Hotham Arms Inn. The route turns left along the road, and then turns right at the
T-junction.

Follow the road to a crossroads. Go straight ahead along the narrower road which eventually turns sharp right. Go past the bridleway junction on the left and continue along the sandy bridleway track, turning right at the T-junction to return to Hotham. Keep ahead when you reach a road, going along Main Street and passing **St Oswald's Church** and a superb **old barn**. Next, walk past – or pause at – the Hotham Arms, on the left. The road now bears sharply left and right to reach the junction with the narrower road met earlier. Go through the entrance to, and follow the drive through, Hotham Hall's grounds, passing close to the Hall on the left. Take a moment to have a look at the bell.

As you leave the drive, turn to look at the **notice** on the southern wall of the lodge. Now keep straight ahead, and, if you wish, visit **All Saints' Church** after crossing a bridge over the beck running from the Hotham Hall lake, on the left. Turn right along the side of the beck, taking care to avoid the tree roots. Continue to reach a lovely old mill and there take the path left to reach Church Street, the B1230.

Turn right, passing the Black Swan Inn, and follow the main road left, – as signposted for the M62. Soon, turn right along Westgate to return to the start, just past the White Hart Inn.

POINTS OF INTEREST:

St Oswald's Church and barn – The church was founded in 1278. Read the plaque on the nearby barn.

Notice (at Hotham Hall) – The notice is a reminder of World War I and is well worth reading.

All Saints' Church – The church was founded in 1175 and is a reminder of the ancient history of the village. It is worth exploring inside.

REFRESHMENTS:

The Hotham Arms, on the route.
The Black Swan Inn, North Cave.
The White Hart Inn, North Cave.

Walk 56   HULL BRIDGE   5m (8km)

Maps: OS Sheets Landranger 107; Pathfinder 676 and 687.

Easy walking, mainly along field tracks and riverbank.

Start: At 056417, the east side of Hull Bridge, near the Crown and Anchor Inn.

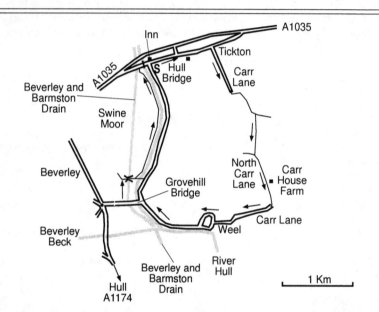

Walk back towards the access road and go ahead into Tickton. Go past St Paul's Church and the village hall and then turn right, just before the chapel, to go along Carr Lane. Keep ahead as this becomes rougher at first and then, soon, becomes a grass track. Cross a wooden bridge and turn left alongside a drain, soon turning right along a narrow grass track between fields. Follow the track to reach a wider farm track. Turn left and, in a few yards, turn right at a junction.

As you pass through a gateway, the track becomes North Carr Lane and passes Carr House Farm: continue along the wider track which becomes Carr Lane as it turns right at a junction, and follow it into Weel. Keep ahead, now walking along a surfaced road which passes several bungalows. Soon after the road turns sharp left to reach Weel Road.

Turn right along the road, heading towards Beverley. The road follows the curving bank of the **River Hull**. When a public amenity site is reached, the embankment widens and a narrow path on it enables you to leave the road. On the opposite bank is the lock entry to Beverley Beck. A motley assortment of small boats are moored along the river side. Continue to reach and cross the lifting Grovehill Bridge over the river. Here you can divert to see **Beverley Beck** by immediately turning left along the riverside, taking care not to trip over the mooring ropes. The wide track narrows and bears right to reach the beck. The walk can again be extended by walking around both ends of the beck: retrace your steps to Grovehill bridge.

From the bridge, walk a short distance towards Beverley, crossing Barmston Drain, then turn right, alongside the drain, passing industrial premises for a short distance before reaching a large footbridge. Here, cross the drain and soon turn left to cross a stile. You are now on **Swine Moor Common**. Turn right, close to the Common's boundary, to gain the western embankment of the River Hull. Turn left, and follow the riverbank, passing further moored boats to arrive back at Hull Bridge. Cross this modern footbridge to return to the starting point close to the Crown and Anchor Inn.

POINTS OF INTEREST:

River Hull – The river is navigable and tidal here and small boats frequently pass. Trawlers and other small ships were once built in Beverley close to the Beck.

Beverley Beck – Barges used to enter through the lock. It is nearly a mile long, and now used mainly for fishing.

Swine Moor Common – This is one of the beautiful commons of Beverley. It is in the care of the Pasture Masters and is mainly grazed by horses and cattle.

REFRESHMENTS:

The Crown and Anchor Inn, Hull Bridge.
There is also plenty of choice in Beverley.

Walk 57　　　　　**KEYINGHAM**　　　　　5m (8km)

Maps: OS Sheets Landranger 107; Pathfinder 697.
Gentle walking along field paths and a disused railway line.
Start: At 245255, St Nicholas Church, Keyingham.

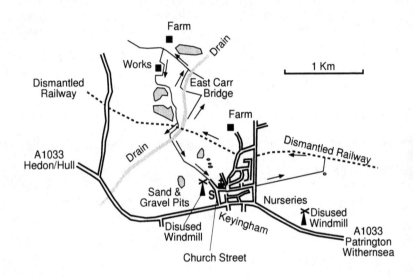

Take the footpath on the south side of the church and follow it to a road. Bear right at the junction and, soon, turn left. Now keep straight ahead along Wauldby Garth Road to reach a T-junction. Go straight over and follow a footpath that goes past a cemetery and soon enters an open field with a drain on the right. There are views of Ottringham and Patrington churches, as well as a disused windmill, to the right from here. Continue to a pond at the field corner and turn left there to reach the disused **Hull-Withernsea railway**. Turn left, heading back towards the Keyingham. A privately-owned section of the disused line near the village means that you must turn right along a track and, on reaching a wider lane, turn left down it. Keep left at the next junction and, soon, turn right to regain the old line.

　　　Now, when a bridge takes the railway over a wide drain, note the footpath on the left, but turn right opposite it, going along a wide, though rough track with the drain on

106

your right. Follow the track left at a drain junction and, soon, follow the clear, but narrower, path bearing right, going through an open field, along the side of a drain.

Where the path reaches a wider track (East Carr Road) to the left of a bridge, turn left, along the track, passing a wooded area on the right. A pond may be visible through the trees. Totley Farm also comes into view, through the trees, just before you reach their end. Here, a narrower track goes off to the left: follow this, with a hedge on your right, to arrive at an untidy works area. There is a metal gate across its access road to the left: cross the metal stile on the right-hand side of the gate and follow the road beyond. The road reaches an area of woodland and, as it bears left, passes the side of a **large pond** now used for fishing.

Immediately past the pond, turn right, off the road, through a gap in a wooden fence. Now keep to the narrow grass track, with the pond quite close on your right. There is a swampy area, with trees, on the left: when you reach a small open area, bear left along a narrow footpath which goes between bushes, heading towards the left-hand side of a second pond. Continue to reach a stile near the corner of the pond. Cross, follow the track beyond past a building and, soon, bear a little left to rejoin the disused railway.

Turn left, back towards the drain bridge. When the bridge is reached, do not cross: instead, turn right, alongside the drain, and walk to the nearby footbridge. Cross and walk straight ahead, following the clear path across the field to reach an enclosed track. Continue along the track back into Keyingham. Go past a gravel quarry and a converted windmill as you enter the village and walk ahead to return to the church.

POINTS OF INTEREST:

Hull-Withernsea Railway – Unfortunately much of the line has been lost to walkers, but from Keyingham it provides a bridleway into Hull.

Large pond – Excavation, particularly of sand and gravel, has left a number of ponds in the area. These are now used mainly for fishing, though water skiing also may be seen on the second pond.

REFRESHMENTS:

The Ship Inn, Main Street, Keyningham.
The Blue Bell Inn, Main Street, Keyningham.

EASINGTON

5m (8km)
or 7m ($11^1/_4$km)

Maps: OS Sheets Landranger 113; Pathfinder 709.
Gentle walking between sea and river. Exposed in bad weather.
Start: At 399192, All Saints' Church, Easington.

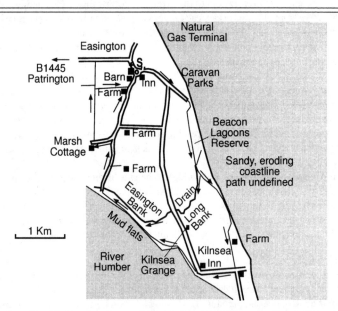

Walk along Seaside Road, going straight on where the Kilnsea road turns right to reach the cliff top. Turn right and, soon, bear right to the **Nature Reserve** notice. Cross the low wall (New Bank) alongside the lagoons, and continue along the grass track beyond to reach its junction with the deep drain alongside Long Bank.

The shorter route turns right here to follow the path along the southern side of the drain. Cross the Kilnsea road and continue until an enclosed area of bushes is reached. Turn left, passing them, to reach the River Humber's bank. Turn right, rejoining the longer route.

For the longer route, descend and bear left to reach the sea shore. Soon, bear right along a wide, rough track, following it to reach the Kilnsea to Spurn road. Turn right, go past small St Helen's Church and continue along the road to reach the **River Humber** close to the Crown and Anchor Inn. Turn right and descend to the riverbank. Ahead now, the shore line bears left and a track begins on the top of the embankment: follow this to reach an the enclosed area of bushes where the shorter route is rejoined.

The combined walk continues along the riverbank track. Go through a metal gate and descend, then take the lane to the right which leads back towards **Easington**. Go past a narrow lane on the right to reach a lane on the left. The shorter route continues ahead here, following the lane back into Easington. Keep to the left of the church to pass the lovely thatched tithe barn before returning to the start.

The longer route turns left, along the lane and, a short distance before reaching Marsh Cottage, the building ahead, turns right along a wide green lane. Follow the lane up a slight hill and, at the top, look right to see a farm with a large grain silo. A hedge line alongside fields leads towards this. Turn right, along a footpath, with the hedge on your left, to reach a stile on the left-hand side of the farm. Beware nettles! Cross and follow the path beyond along the side of the farm to reach the lane to Easington down which walkers on the shorter route have travelled. Note that the the the nearby exit from the farm may be an easier way of regaining the lane. Turn left along the lane to return to the start.

POINTS OF INTEREST:

Nature Reserve – This is the Beacon Lagoons Reserve, which is subject to sea flooding due to the eroding shore. It is a summer home to little terns.

The River Humber – The river has extensive mudflats here which, sheltered by the disappearing Spurn Head, support a wide variety of wading birds. It is also England's busiest river for shipping.

Easington – The village is the home of a large natural gas terminal. All Saints' Church is worth exploring.

REFRESHMENTS:

The Crown and Anchor Inn, at Kilnsea.
There is also a good choice in Easington.

Walk 60   **BRANSTON** $5\frac{1}{4}$m ($8\frac{1}{2}$km)

Maps: OS Sheets Landranger 121; Pathfinder 782.

A pretty village and the Lincoln Heath: lakes and aeroplanes.

Start: At 022673, Branston Church.

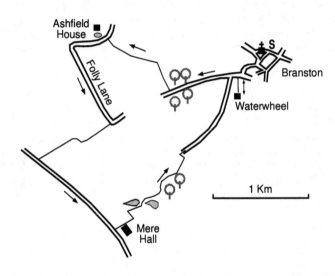

A very short part of this walk is on Pathfinder sheet 781. If you haven't got it, don't worry - you won't get lost without it. There is a small parking area opposite the church in **Branston**. If this is full try Hall Lane, which is on the walk.

Facing the church, set off to your left and walk through to Hall Lane. Turn right, and right again at the junction with Thackers Lane. As you walk out of the village, Branston Hall can be seen on the right. After 500 yards, at the corner of some woods, turn right near a pylon and a bridleway sign.

    Go down the track by the woodland and bear right to reach stepping stones over the stream. Here, turn left by the stream until you reach the farm road near Ashfield House. Turn left again and follow the farm road to reach a metalled road (Folly Lane). Keep straight ahead along the lane, but where it bends sharply left, turn right along a track, following it to reach another road. On this section of the walk there is a good view northwards to Lincoln cathedral. You may also have close up views of RAF AWACs as they take-off and land at **Waddington Airfield**.

Turn left along the road. As you near Mere Hall Farm there is a signed track on the left: take this. The track bends left by some conifers, then sharply right before passing between two lakes. By the second lake, just beyond a small brick shed, turn left down the bank and go over a footbridge. Turn right and keep to the field edge around the woodland. When a large notice board is seen up to your left, walk up to it to join a farm track. Follow the track back to the edge of Branston where the outward route is met. Now make a 200 yard detour into Waterwheel Lane on the right to see **The Waterwheel** before retracing your steps to the start.

POINTS OF INTEREST:

Branston – The 'old' part of the village has steep streets with stone houses and cottages. It is known that there was a Roman settlement here and the church has a Saxon tower, though the rest was rebuilt after a fire in 1963. At the old Bertie Arms (passed on the walk) a plaque records the meeting on 26th May 1765 to organise the 'Enclosures' in the parish.

Waddington Airfield – Waddington is an RAF AWAC (Airborne Warfare and Control System) base, the aircraft, with their odd-shaped radar pods, operating from one of the county's major airfields. The station opened in 1916 and was later home to squadrons of Vulcan 'V' bombers. The runway extends over the Roman Ermine Street. **The Waterwheel** – Recently restored this was originally built to supply Branston Hall, Longhills Hall, (south-east of the village) and a few other houses of the gentry with their domestic water. It may have had a wooden wheel at first. The present metal one, installed in 1879, has had both gas and petrol engines to power it, and is known to have been in working order as late as the 1950s.

REFRESHMENTS:
The Waggon and Horses, Branston.

111

Walk 61   **BOSTON AND THE HAVEN**   5¹/₄m (8¹/₂km)
Maps: OS Sheets Landranger 131; Pathfinders 816 and 837.
*A short walk of historic interest: birds, boats and views over The
Wash.*
Start: At 359403, the Haven Country Park and picnic area.

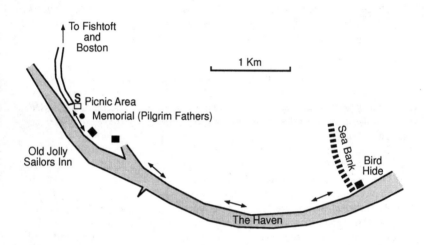

To reach the start, take the Fishtoft road from **Boston**. In Fishtoft take the Cut End road
by the Red Cow Inn. Bear right at the fork by the old Wesleyan chapel. This narrow lane
ends at the picnic site. The walk could be shortened by keeping left at the chapel, there
being limited parking at grid reference 380393. Take binoculars and consult local tide
tables. If you go at high tide there will usually be a variety of shipping, both fishing
boats and larger vessels, to see at close hand entering or leaving Boston docks.

Go through the gate by the picnic site at the **Pilgrim Fathers Memorial** and walk along
the haven bank. Keep to the bank top until you reach the Old Jolly Sailors, once a
waterside inn. Pass in front of this and continue to an Anglian River Authority pumping
station.

Just beyond the pumping station there is a footpath sign. Turn right along this signed path, again keeping to the bank as it initially veers away from the river: it soon rejoins the waters edge. All that remains then is to follow the bank for about $1\frac{1}{2}$ miles to its end where a **Bird Hide** overlooks The Wash.

To return, simply retrace the outward route.

POINTS OF INTEREST:

Boston – In medieval times Boston was second only to London as a trading port. International trade was then with Europe, but later, as Atlantic routes developed, Boston's prosperity declined. Silting up of the Haven added to the problems. Its major export was wool, for which Lincolnshire was renowned, and an important import was wine. The magnificent parish church – the famous Boston 'Stump' – reflects the wealth of the local merchants. However, there was an improvement after 1884 when the dock was built and the Haven made deeper and wider. Today Boston is a busy port importing mainly steel, grain and timber.

The Pilgrim Fathers – The picnic site is at Scotia Creek. From here one group of the religious separatists known as the Pilgrim Fathers first set sail in September 1607. They were captured in this attempt to reach Holland and imprisoned. Their cells can be seen in the Guildhall Museum in Boston. They later escaped to the continent from Immingham and went on to America via Plymouth in the *Mayflower*. A detailed history is given on information boards near the Memorial Stone.

Bird Hide – For ornithologists there is a bird hide at the seaward end of the Haven bank. From it the waders and wildfowl of The Haven can be seen.

REFRESHMENTS:

None en route, but there is a wide choice in Boston, while the *Red Cow*, Fishtoft, is a little closer.

Walk 62   **THE THEDDLETHORPES** $5\frac{1}{4}$m ($8\frac{1}{2}$km)

Maps: OS Sheets Landranger 113; Pathfinder 749.

Escape the holiday crowds with this walk over dunes, marsh, fields and quiet country roads.

Start: At 483892, the car park, Brickyard Lane, Theddlethorpe St Helen.

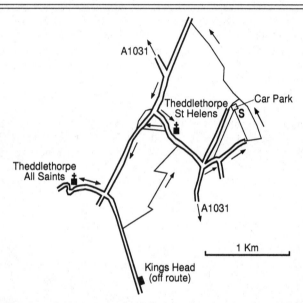

When approaching Theddlethorpe St Helens on the A1031 from the south two lanes go right together at GR 479885. Brickyard Lane is the left-hand one, at the end of which there is an English Nature car park.

From the car park walk over the **Nature Reserve** to the beach and turn left along the foreshore. At a red warning triangle and a flagpost, turn left inland, passing another car park, and walk to the main A1031. Keep forward to the junction with Station Road and bear left. (Or walk up Station Road and visit St Helens church later.) On the bend by **Theddlethorpe St Helen's Church** a footpath is signed to the right: cross a stile and a footbridge into a large grass field. Now aim just right of Manor House Farm and, beyond another stile and footbridge, join **Station Road**. Turn left and walk to a crossroads. (To visit **Theddlethorpe All Saints' Church**, you should turn right here.)

Turn left into Mill Road (or keep straight on if you are returning from the church), and take a signed footpath on the left just before the telephone box. (The King's Head is further along the road, a 1 mile round trip.) Follow the field edge with a dyke on your left, then bear left to pass behind a derelict house. Turn right over a footbridge and then walk ahead towards a white house and St Helen's Church amongst trees in the distance. Go left at the waymarkers, then right through a metal gate. A grass track then leads to the road near the church. Turn right and walk to the junction with Brickyard Lane and Sea Lane. Go down Sea Lane, but when it bends to the right, keep ahead along a farm road. Go through the farm, cross a paddock and a stile, and walk out to the foreshore again. Turn left and, after about 500 yards, watch carefully for the track back to the start.

POINTS OF INTEREST:

The Nature Reserve – Notice boards at the car park describe the Reserve, its wildlife and management. In mid/late June wild orchids can be seen here.

Theddlethorpe St Helen's Church – The church was much rebuilt by the Victorians but still has a 14th-century stone reredos.

The nearby coast was a favourite holiday haunt of the writer D H Lawrence, Theddlethorpe being mentioned in his diaries. His first visit was in 1906.

Modern technological architecture is seen to the south in the shape of the Viking Gas Terminal. Opened in 1972, it is jointly run by Conoco (who produce and pipe in North Sea gas) and British Gas (who distribute and sell it).

Station Road – The walk crosses the dismantled line of the Louth and East Coast Railway. This was opened in 1877 and closed in 1961.

Theddlethorpe All Saints' Church – Known in the area as the 'Cathedral of the Marshes', and the largest of the many magnificent marshland churches, the church stands isolated, a patchwork of multi-coloured stone and brickwork. Inside there is much old woodwork, including a rood screen. There is another rare stone reredos here too. Now redundant, and locked, most of the interior can be seen through the large, clear glass windows. (An address for the key is displayed for those wishing to make another visit after the walk.)

REFRESHMENTS:

None on the walk, but *The Kings Head* (472871) can be reached by the short extension mentioned in the text.

There are also possibilities in Saltfleet, 5 miles to the north and Mablethorpe, 4 miles to the south.

Walk 63 STAMFORD AND EASTON-ON-THE-HILL 5½m (8¾km)

Maps: OS Sheets Landranger 141; Pathfinder 897.

A walk between an historic town and a beautiful village.

Start: At 028068, the car park, Station Road, Stamford.

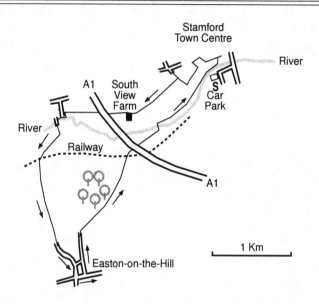

There is a charge for the car park: reach it by turning into Station Road near the famous George Hotel. One warning too! The outward route crosses the A1 dual carriageway. Even though visibility is good in both directions, and there is a pedestrian gap in the central barrier, DO TAKE YOUR TIME AND TAKE CARE!

From the car park entrance turn left, cross a footbridge and go over the Meadows towards **Stamford** town centre. After a second footbridge, turn left along Bath Row. (The old public baths can still be seen.) Bear right into Kings Mill Lane, turn left into Austin Street and take the next left downhill to join the quaintly named Melancholy Walk. At a gate and stile turn right up a track for 150 yards, going left at a signpost along another track between allotments to reach open fields. Go straight over the first field, continuing along a headland to South View Farm. Turn right, then left into the farmyard. The farmer's 'white feet' signs will now guide you through the buildings. Continue with a fence/hedge on your right.

Cross the A1, WITH CARE, and follow the signed footpath opposite, heading towards the cement works in the distance and, closer, a large house with conspicuous chimneys. Turn left along a lane and where this becomes a private road, keep left along a fenced path which veers right by the river to reach a bridge. Cross and walk beside a fence to join, and follow, a wide green lane on the right. Cross the railway and continue up to **Easton-on-the-Hill**. Walk up West Street, turn left into High Street and left again into Church Street. Beyond the church, turn right on to the **Jurassic Way**. Cross two fields and follow a track which descends steadily beside woods to reach a footbridge and steps where the railway is re-crossed. After a second footbridge over the river there is a tunnel under the A1. Continue to another footbridge, cross, and return to the start over the meadows by the river. On the way you will pass the site of the **Roman Ford.**

POINTS OF INTEREST:

Stamford – As the best preserved stone-built town in England it was the first Conservation Area created in 1967. Its history has seen the coming, and going, of Romans, Saxons, and Danes, for whom it was a capital under the Danelaw. Medieval prosperity, based on the wealth of wool merchants, declined, but the stage coach era on 'The Great North Road' revived the town's fortunes.

On the edge of the town (actually in Cambridgeshire as Stamford lies close to the border of that county as well as to Leicestershire and Northamptonshire) is Burghley House, the fabulous Elizabethan mansion of Lord Burghley (William Cecil) who was chief minister to Queen Elizabeth I. It is home to the annual Burghley Horse Trials.

Easton-on-the-Hill – The village is just in Northamptonshire: it is difficult to walk far from Stamford without crossing a county boundary! Like Stamford, its beautiful stone buildings are of the local honey coloured limestone, the type of stone famous in Bath and the Cotswolds. The church has part of a painted stone reredos and a George VI coat-of-arms.

The Jurassic Way – This long distance path crosses Northamptonshire to end in Stamford. The waymarkers have a distinctive fossil logo.

Roman Ford – The Roman road from London to York crossed the river here. In 61 AD the 9th legion were chased over it by Boedecea.

REFRESHMENTS:

There is ample opportunity in both Stamford and Easton-on-the-Hill.

Walk 64   **MARTON AND THE TRENT**   5$^1/_2$m (8$^3/_4$km)

Maps: OS Sheets Landranger 121; Pathfinder 746.

An easy figure of eight on country lanes and the river bank.

Start: At 840818, Marton Church.

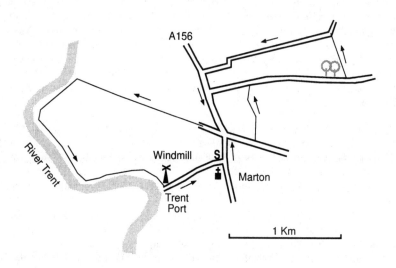

Park in Trent Port Lane. Marton, close to the church. The first section of this walk, part of which is on a permissive path, could be omitted to approximately halve the distance.

Turn left along the main road from **Marton Church** and walk to the **Black Swan** at the cross-roads. Turn left here if you are walking the shorter route.

    Otherwise, go right up Stow Park Road for 250 yards, then take a footpath to the left. This passes behind some houses before becoming a grass track: follow it to reach a metalled lane. Turn right. In summer this lane is lined with a profusion of wild roses. After about 1,000 yards, the lane bends past a small woodland on the left. At the far corner of this, look carefully in the hedge on the left for an unsigned plank footbridge over a ditch. Cross and walk beside the woods and then forward along the field edge to meet a farm lane at a corner. Turn left and follow the lane to reach the main A156 road. There are pleasant countryside views and, before the lane drops steeply to the main road, a good view of **Gate Burton House** and its church.

Cross the main road with great care, and turn left along the footpath beside it to return to Marton. On reaching the Black Swan again, turn right into **Littleborough Lane**. The lane soon becomes a tree-lined track: follow it to the **River Trent**. A large farmhouse, apparently at the end of the lane, is suddenly and spectacularly revealed to be on the opposite bank. Downstream the view includes The Chateau (see Points of Interest).

Cross a stile on the left and walk upstream beside the river, crossing further stiles. When the river swings to the right in a great horseshoe, towards a ruined windmill, look on your left for a stile by some trees. Cross this and walk to the right, behind the trees, to reach a second stile. Ascend some steps to a third stile, cross and walk parallel to the river, but now high above it, to reach a fourth stile near the windmill. A short track now leads to the end of a tarmac lane. This is **Trent Port**. From here you turn left to return to Marton, but first, enjoy a final view of the river far below from the nearby lifebelt.

POINTS OF INTEREST:
Marton Church – Dedicated to St Margaret of Antioch it has some wonderful Saxon herringbone masonry.
The Black Swan – Now a guest house, this was originally a coaching inn: the large archway can still be seen. There is a local legend that Dick Turpin stayed here.
Gate Burton House – This was built in the 1770s. The old school is now a private house. Between the river and the main road stands a folly, the Gate Burton Chateau. This now belongs to the Landmark Trust and is rented as holiday accommodation.
Littleborough Lane – The Roman road of Tillbridge Lane leaves Ermine Street just north of Lincoln. At Marton it becomes Littleborough Lane leading to the Trent where there was once a ford to Littleborough Fort on the far bank. Occasionally at low water the large stones of the ford can still be seen.
The River Trent – Even this far from the sea the Trent is a tidal river, and has a tidal bore – similar to that on the River Severn, and known locally as The Aegir – for which the National Rivers Authority publish a timetable, obtainable from the Tourist Information Centre in Gainsborough.
Trent Port – The river was once a busy commercial waterway. The windmill at Trent Port was built in 1799 and there were warehouses and a wharf here too.

REFRESHMENTS:
The Ingleby Arms, Marton.
The Black Swan, Marton, also has a dining room and tea gardens open to non-residents.

Walk 65   BARHOLM AND BRACEBOROUGH   5¹/₂m (8³/₄ km)

Maps: OS Sheets Landranger 130; Pathfinder 877.

Three mellowed stone villages by easy field and woodland paths.

Start: At 089109, in Barholm.

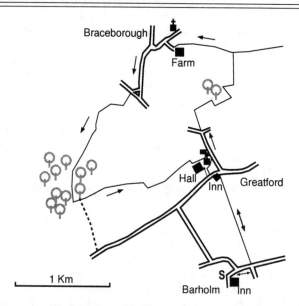

These villages are tucked away amongst the back roads between fenland and the wooded hills rising towards Stamford. Parking in Barholm is limited but try in the lane leading to the inn.

Walk to the church and take the path on the left by the churchyard. This makes a bee-line for Greatford, crossing the Greatford Cut drain on the way and, after a farmyard, emerges in **Greatford** itself. Turn left and pass the inn. Turn right into the entrance of Greatford Hall, cross the West Glen River, walking ahead to the church to see the **Rev. Dr Francis Willis** memorial. Leave the churchyard by the path from the north-east corner. Turn left at a road and, when this bends left, take the fieldpath straight ahead. At the field corner, bear right. Pass a footbridge and go along the headland to skirt three sides of a small wood. Cross the next footbridge on your left. Go across a field, heading roughly for the second pylon and another footbridge seen near trees, but when a farm track is met, turn left towards **Braceborough**. Bear right through the farm, then go left, and left again in the village. At a triangular road junction, bear right, before crossing to a footpath. The path rises beside trees to reach a waymarker and a sleeper bridge on your right. Cross the next field diagonally, aiming to the left of three large trees on the far side. Cross a second field, again diagonally, in the same direction. Across a third field a footpath signpost is now visible near woods. From it, turn left along a track to another signpost 50 yards away.

Turn left to a stile and bear right across grass to another. Walk across an arable field, keeping well left of two large oak trees in the middle. Once over a grassy bridge into another field, veer diagonally right to its far corner, then follow a headland on the right to a stile into woods. Turn left through the woods to reach a footbridge on the right. Cross and walk beside a fence, following waymarkers around the gardens of some new houses, before turning left along a gravel drive. At the road, turn right into Greatford. Now retrace the outward route back to **Barholm**.

POINTS OF INTEREST:

Greatford – The river was once diverted for a mill. It originally took a more direct course north of the church to the 'ford' from which the village derives its name. The 'old' Hall burned down in 1922 but was rebuilt. Carvings scattered around the village (crowns, elephants, etc) were the work of Col Fitzwilliams, an occupant of the hall in the 1930s. As you approach the church note that the tower is to your right, forming a transept, and not in its usual place at the west end.

Rev. Dr Francis Willis (1718-1807) – Originally from Lincoln, he pioneered the treatment of the mentally ill, founding an asylum at Greatford, and went on to achieve considerable fame after his treatment of King George III. His monument, in the north transept, was commissioned by his sons, and carved by the famous sculptor Joseph Nollekens.

Braceborough – It is hard to appreciate now that this was once a thriving spa. Although activity ceased by the 1940s a road sign (north-west of the village and just off the walk) still points to 'Braceborough Spa'.

Barholm – A quiet and secluded spot. The church has features from Saxon and Norman through to Victorian times, and is dedicated to a very early saint, St Martin of Tours, born in Hungary about 315.

REFRESHMENTS:
The Five Horseshoes, Barholm.
The Hare and Hounds, Greatford.

Walk 66   **IRBY DALES AND SWALLOW**   5³/₄m (9¹/₄km)

Maps: OS Sheets Landranger 113; Pathfinder 719.

Unsuspected tranquillity a stone's throw from the A46.

Start: At 195049, near Irby-upon-Humber church.

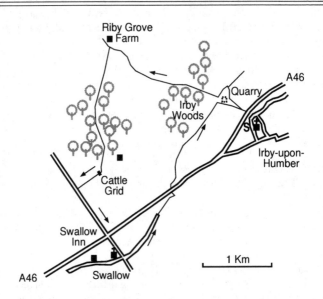

Irby-upon-Humber lies close to the outskirts of Grimsby and is bypassed by the A46.
Turn off into the village and find the parking area near the church. This has easy access
to the main road, which has to be crossed to reach the Dales.

Cross the A46, with great care, and, almost opposite, cross a stile to the left of a house
and follow the footpath beyond, walking beside a hedge, away from the main road.
Beyond a second stile a track develops: this veers right and down to the valley bottom.
On meeting another track, turn left and walk to a pair of gates. The track ahead is your
return route.

  Immediately through the gates, turn right to follow an obvious path uphill into Irby
Woods. Ignoring all side paths and tracks, walk through the woods following a farm
track on the far side to walk over the hill beyond. Descend steeply to Riby Grove Farm.

Just before the farm, turn left at a signpost to go along a grass track. The track leads into 'The Vale'. In this beautiful, wooded valley, keep left where the track divides. At the end of the woods there is a stile: cross the field beyond to reach a fence and another stile and signpost. Cross and turn right along a farm road, going over a cattle grid. Walk uphill to the public road.

Go left and re-cross the A46, again with great care, continuing down into **Swallow**. (From the cross-roads the Swallow Inn is 300 yards to your right, past the church.) To continue the walk, turn left, following the old road to its terminus where it is possible to continue ahead zig-zagging past small plantations of new trees to reach the new road again. About 20 yards away is a layby: from this cross the A46 again and turn right along a hidden loop of the old road.

From this old road a track goes off to the left: follow this back to the double gates mentioned earlier. After these, bear right immediately along a rising track past the face of an old chalk quarry. Now go left, uphill, to rejoin the outward route.

POINTS OF INTEREST:
The main object of this walk is to explore the peace and quiet of the Irby Dales area, its attractions being within easy access of the Humber Bank conurbations.
Irby-upon-Humber – There was a settlement here at least as far back as Norman times. Parts of the church date from then, but internally it was restored in the 1880s. Irby's long name is necessary to distinguish from the other (longer named) Irby-in-the-Marsh further south in the county.
Swallow – There are similarities with Irby here. Mentioned in the Domesday Book as *Sualun*, it has a church that is Norman in parts and of ancient appearance, but restored. Since the building of the new road it too has regained a tranquillity first lost with the advent of the automobile.

REFRESHMENTS:
The Swallow Inn, Swallow.
There is a Little Chef roadhouse at the A461/A18 roundabout just over $^3/_4$ mile from the start, at 206058.

Walk 67   **WOLD NEWTON AND BEESBY**   6m (9½km)

Maps: OS Sheets Landranger 113; Pathfinder 731.

A beautiful Wolds walk.

Start: At 246971 on a wide grass verge 250 yards up the Grainsby Lane.

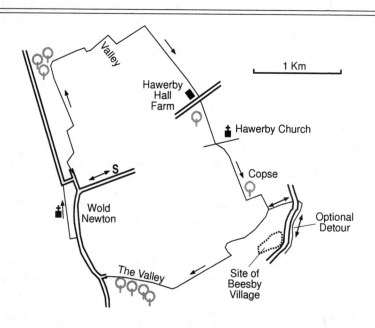

This walk explores unspoilt Wold countryside and is well waymarked. Footpaths in the area have recently been re-routed and may not correspond to those shown on old maps.

Walk back downhill and turn right. At the first bend, go ahead along a waymarked track. Bear right, uphill, after passing a small quarry and then walk left beside a hedge. Keep forward as the path cuts through the hedge and continue to the corner of some woods. Go ahead, then right uphill, continuing until the path dips into a wooded valley and rises again to an old gate. There, turn right and then left in the field corner. After a further 400 yards, at a signpost, turn right along a track to Hawerby Hall Farm, going through to reach a minor road. Cross and walk to the right, behind a house, then left along the field edge by the woods. Go right, through the hedge, and walk by the side of a garden to reach a track junction. Turn left, and then right opposite the house gateway. (The ruined **Hawerby Church** is in the trees just to the left.) Keep forward to reach a copse, turning left beyond it and then going right at the next waymarker to reach the edge of Beesby Wood.

(Here, a detour left, and then right along the road for 800 yards, will bring you to the site of **Beesby**, a 'lost' village. Return along the same route.)

Turn right beside the wood and, at the end, at a small gate, go left, downhill. At a second gate, go right then walk ahead beside a wire fence. Go through two sets of gates, then again walk beside a wire fence to reach more woods. This is The Valley. Veer right into the trees and walk to a road.

Turn right, go past a lake and, at the edge of **Wold Newton**, take the path on the left opposite the second house. At the top of the paddock turn right and follow the path across the front of the churchyard, continuing through a farmyard to reach a road. Turn right to return to the start.

POINTS OF INTEREST:

Hawerby Church – A sad, derelict church with cracked walls and a collapsing roof.
Beesby – One of many abandoned villages in the Wolds. Without the detour described a glimpse of the site can still be had from the southern end of Beesby Woods (at grid reference 261963) where medieval ridge and furrow fields are evident. There are squirrels about too!
Wold Newton – A quiet village, almost secretive, hidden away in its isolated valley. The only way to the church from any direction is by fieldpath. In the porch an ancient notice board tells of the duties of churchwardens, including assigning seats with special provisions for the poor.

REFRESHMENTS:

None en route. The nearest are:
The Clickem Inn, at grid reference 222973 on the Binbrook road, $1^1/_4$ miles to the west.
The Plough Inn, Binbrook.

Walk 68   BLANKNEY BARFF AND THE CAR DYKE   6m (9¹/₂km)

Maps: OS Sheets Landranger 121; Pathfinder 782.

This level walk visits a deserted World War II airfield and the Roman Car Dyke.

Start: At 112615, the north-east corner of the airfield perimeter road.

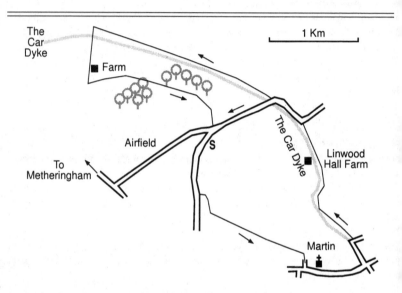

To reach the start, drive east from Metheringham. Turn left at the road junction at GR 101608 to cross the old airfield. Park where the main perimeter road is met. The stretch of road through Martin village is on Pathfinder map 798 which is not essential to navigation. A short-cut is given in the route instructions reducing the distance to 4 miles (6¹/₄km).

From the parking area, walk 700 yards southwards along the **Metheringham Airfield** perimeter road. At a waymarker turn left. (An RAF memorial is a few paces further on.) After 100 yards, turn right behind a hedge and an empty house. Join a green track near a brick barn and follow this to reach a metalled lane which leads into Martin near the church.

Turn left through the village and, at the crossroads at the far end of the village, turn left again. At a right-hand bend, go ahead along a grass track, walking beside the **Car Dyke**. Do not cross the concrete bridge: instead, continue along the track, bearing right with the dyke as you approach Linwood Hall Farm. Bear left over a stile to join a track and follow it, still walking parallel to the water.

(When a road joins on the left take it for a short-cut return to the start.)

The route continues beside the Car Dyke for another $1^1/_4$ miles, the track becoming a concrete private road. Just beyond Moonacre House, look down the bank on the right for a welcoming carved wooden seat. Continue to the track junction at GR 098625, turning left, uphill, there. Go past Metheringham Barff Farm, then turn left again along a farm road. On the approach to some woods, waymarkers lead you on a short dog-leg, first right, then left. Pass the woods and walk straight ahead over the airfield to return to the start.

POINTS OF INTEREST:

On the map the area is named Blankney Barff, and there are other *barffs* hereabouts. Barff is an old Lincolnshire word for *a hill running along by low ground.*

Metheringham Airfield – The airfield was built in only a few months from the end of 1942 to autumn 1943. Farmers were given 48 hours notice to abandon their homes and land before work began. By November 1943, 106 Squadron had arrived. Eventually some 2,000 people were stationed here. It was closed in less than $2^1/_2$ years shortly after the end of the war.

There is a Visitor Centre at nearby Westmoor Farm open on summer weekends or by appointment. In addition, North Mesteven Council have published an Airfield Trail – obtainable from Tourist Offices – with detailed histories of this and other airfields in the vicinity.

The Car Dyke – This 'canal' is thought to be of Roman construction. It cleverly follows the contours of the countryside and links the River Nene, near Peterborough, with the River Witham east of Lincoln, a distance of 75 miles. Its primary use is thought to have been for transport, though it also served as a drain by diverting water flowing from the hills to the west away from the fenlands of the Witham valley. There are numerous Roman settlements along its length.

Recently a project has begun to enliven the course of the dyke by placing sculptures beside it: you should see at least two on the walk.

REFRESHMENTS:

The Royal Oak, Martin.

There are also several inns in Metheringham.

Walk 69   **WELLINGORE TO COLEBY**   6½m (10½km)

Maps: OS Sheets Landranger 121; Pathfinders 781 and 797.

An easy, but dramatic, section of the Viking Way, passing through four picturesque stone villages.

Start: At 983566, Hall Street, Wellingore.

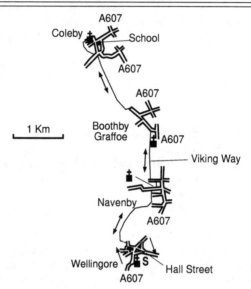

Although this is in essence a 'there and back' walk no apology is needed: the views, magnificent throughout, can withstand a second scrutiny from the fresh perspective provided by the return journey. Brief detours are described into the beautiful stone-built villages to give variety. The Viking Way is well waymarked with its helmet logo.

Walk down Hall Street to the corner by the church. Almost opposite is Vicarage Lane. Walk down it, taking the first right turn, then going left and right in quick succession to reach Memorial Hall Drive. At the hall, turn left by a childrens' play area to a kissing gate in a wall. Cross some rough grass then bear right on the far side of a high hedge. At the edge of **Navenby**, the path meets the end of a lane near a pond: turn left here, down The Smoots, on a narrow path. At a metal kissing gate turn right to another a few yards away, soon reaching a stile on the left. Cross this and the field beyond to another stile on to a road. A few paces uphill, climb some stone steps to reach the churchyard. Walk up past the church and turn left into The Catwalk. When this ends at a road (North Lane), the Viking Way continues a little to the left on the opposite side. Follow it to **Boothby Graffoe**.

Walk through the village and into Far End, following it to a stile at its end. Cross the paddock beyond, going diagonally left to another stile. Turn right and walk to **Coleby**, reaching the village by the side of a large garden to emerge opposite the Tempest Arms. Turn right, uphill, following Blind Lane. Near the school, turn left. You now have a choice of routes. You can return to the Tempest Arms via High Street, the next left turn, or turn right into Far Lane, passing the Bell Inn to reach a stile at the end. Turn left and follow the path along the edge of the village, again arriving, through an alleyway, at the road by the Tempest Arms.

Cross the road and walk back through Boothby Graffoe and take North Lane into Navenby and turn right along the main road until Clint Lane is reached. Turn right into it and at the end you will reach the pond passed earlier in the day. Now retrace your steps to **Wellingore**, but on leaving Memorial Hall Drive keep left up West Street. Cross the main road, with care, and walk along High Street. Two right turns lead first into Blacksmith Lane and then Hall Street to return to the start.

POINTS OF INTEREST:

Navenby – A wide main street flanked by stone houses, shops and inns. St Peter's church has a magnificent Easter Sepulchre. Also worth seeing are the decorated ceilings and the mosque-like decor in the tower. The churchyard is managed as a nature conservation project: there is an informative display.

Boothby Graffoe – To the west of the village can be seen the remains (now part of a farm) of Somerton Castle. Built in 1281 by Anthony Bek, Bishop of Durham, it was the prison for King John of France in 1359 after his capture at Poitiers by the Black Prince.

Coleby – Look for the unusual conical-shaped stone wellheads in Blind Lane.

Wellingore – The church is of several periods from the 12th century onwards. Nearby is The Hall built by the Neville family in 1750 and extended in 1876. It has a Roman Catholic chapel.

REFRESHMENTS:

The Marquis of Granby, Wellingore.
The Butchers Arms, Navenby.
The Tempest Arms, Coleby.
The Bell Inn, Coleby.

Walk 70   **PARTNEY AND LANGTON**   6¹/₂m (10¹/₂km)

Maps: OS Sheets Landranger 122; Pathfinders 766, 767, 783 and 784.

A walk of historic interest, varied terrain and lots of stiles.

Start: At 411684, near Partney church.

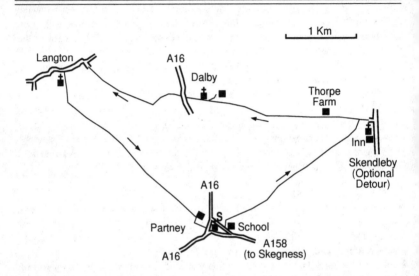

Park just to the north of Partney church. The walk cuts across the corners of four Pathfinder maps, but navigation with the Landranger sheet alone is quite feasible.

Walk away from the church, turn right and take the footpath on the left by the school. At the corner of the school fence, go half-right to an old hedge and waymarker, then slightly left to reach a stile in the field corner. Continue along two field edges with a stream to your left, then, in a long, narrow grass field, veer right to a stile just before a telegraph pole. Skendleby church is now clearly visible: head directly for it, crossing two large fields and going through the hedge between them at two waymarkers to reach a stile by a double fieldgate. Beyond this, a track curves gradually left to a stile on the right below the church. (Beyond the church, up a field, and through the churchyard, is the Blacksmiths Arms.)

The route turns sharp left up the field to reach a stile at the top. Cross overgrown ground under telegraph wires to another stile and then cross rough parkland, staying some 150 yards below Thorpe Farm. Cross a stile in a wire fence to reach a footbridge. Dalby Hall can now be seen ahead: aim just left of it. (It disappears briefly as you cross the next field.) Beyond another bridge, follow a field edge towards Dalby Park. Cross a stile and walk beside a fence for 150 yards, then branch right, uphill, and follow the track from near **Dalby Church** to reach the A16. Cross, with care, and descend a field to a small gate. Turn left and walk diagonally to the far corner of the next field. Go through another gate, then keep directly ahead along a headland and then a farm track, to reach the road at **Langton**. Turn left towards the church, then take the track on the left at the entrance to America Farm. The track soon bends to the left: when it bends sharp left again walk across the field ahead to a 'home-made' stile in a fence. Now towards Partney you will see a group of trees – one taller than the rest – on the far side of the next large field. Walk to these, then go to the left of them. After 100 yards, by a yew tree, follow the track beside the hedge to your right, going around a short dog-leg near The Grange to reach the road at Partney. Visit the churchyard to see the **Matthew Flinders Memorial**, and then return to your car.

POINTS OF INTEREST:
Dalby Church – Built in 1862 in just 4 months! Inside is a picture of the previous church with its thatched roof, and beautiful framed architects drawings for the new one. The Rev Tyler, the vicar in 1801, officiated at the wedding of his step-daughter to Captain Matthew Flinders at Partney.
Langton – The village takes its name from the landowners – the Langton family. Bennet Langton, born in 1737, became a close friend of Dr Samuel Johnson, the compiler of the famous dictionary, who visited Langton on several occasions. The church is an architectural gem, one of the best 18th-century churches in the country, and should not be missed. It has an unusual arrangement of box pews facing into the central aisle and a remarkable three-decker pulpit.
Matthew Flinders Memorial–Matthew Flinders (1774-1814) was born in Donington in south Lincolnshire and became one of the leading navigator/explorers of his day, being the first to circumnavigate Australia. After his marriage he set sail again in July the same year. Enduring shipwreck and imprisonment by the French in Mauritius, he did not return until October 1810.

REFRESHMENTS:
The Blacksmiths Arms, Skendleby.
The Red Lion, Partney.

Walk 71　HATCLIFFE, CUXWOLD AND BEELSBY　7m (11¼km)

Maps: OS Sheets Landranger 113; Pathfinders 719, 720, 730 (and a few yards at the extreme north-west corner of sheet 731). *Good paths, farm tracks and country lanes explore an area of attractive Wolds scenery.*

Start: At 212010, on the lane between Hatcliffe and Beelsby.

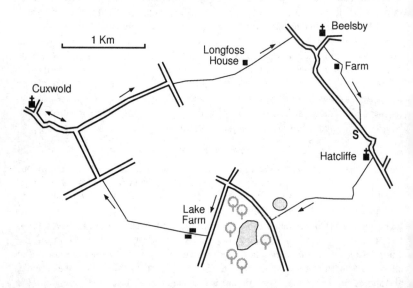

The roadside verges are wide enough to permit parking.

Walk downhill into Hatcliffe and through this picturesque village with cottages clustered along the banks of its stream. Just beyond the church, take the footpath on the right between houses. Go up a pasture, keeping a hedge on your right, and, at a junction with a bridleway, go forward through a handgate, still with a hedge to your right. After a second handgate and a stile, bear sharp right to contour over a long field to a stile in the far left corner. Maintain direction beside a wire fence, cross a stream and continue beside woodland to reach a road at Croxby Pond. Turn right and walk steeply uphill to a crossroads. Turn left, downhill, and then right into Lake Farm. The route now follows part of the **Nev Cole Way**. Once past the farm buildings, take the rising track to the right of a hedge. Where this ends in a V-shaped field corner, turn right, pass through a hedge (there is a waymarker) and walk up the next field on a wide grass strip with a hedge on your right. At a track, keep ahead to reach a road. Turn left for **Cuxwold** and its picturesque church. Then return to this point.

Now keep to the road to reach a T-junction. Cross and take the signed path opposite, going ahead, across a field, to a second signpost. Now follow a grass track down into a valley and up the other side towards the buildings, **Longfoss House**, on the skyline. Join a metalled track and follow this to a road – with outstanding views on a clear day. Turn right and, in Beelsby village, turn left at the road junction. After 100 yards, take the path on the right near a letterbox. Cross a stile and walk past a pond to a second stile near a gate. Now take a track to the left, going behind farm buildings, gradually skirting them, then bearing right to follow waymarkers to a footpath fingerpost. Go left down a valley-shaped field, but halfway along begin to angle up the opposite side to reach a stile in the right-hand corner. Continue beside a fence and conifer wood and, at its corner, veer right to a stile and gate at the road by the start.

POINTS OF INTEREST:

The seclusion found in this corner of the Wolds is the chief attraction of this walk, each village tucked in its own sleepy hollow.

The Nev Cole Way – This long distance path is named for Nev Cole, a local rambler passionate in his love of the outdoors and a champion of walkers rights. He died in 1989 aged 73. In his honour local rambling organisations created a 57-mile walk from the confluence of the River Trent and the Humber along the coast and Wolds.

Cuxwold – In the church is a memorial to Lt Henry Thorold, killed at the Battle of Inkerman in 1884. There are unusual painted and framed biblical texts too.

Longfoss House – The highest point of the walk. The view is spectacular on a clear day. With the naked eye the Yorkshire coast (12 miles) is clearly visible, as is Spurn Head lighthouse (14 miles) and Grimsby dock tower (8 miles). Binoculars will help.

REFRESHMENTS:

None en route, the nearest being:

The Clickem Inn, on the Binbrook to Grimsby road at grid reference 222973.

The Swallow Inn, Swallow, 4 miles to the north-east.

The Plough, Binbrook, 5 miles to the south.

Maps: OS Sheets Landranger 131; Pathfinder 858.

A level figure of eight walk providing extensive views over the fens and marshes.

Start: At 491257, at the road corner near the lighthouse at Guy's Head on the west bank of the River Nene.

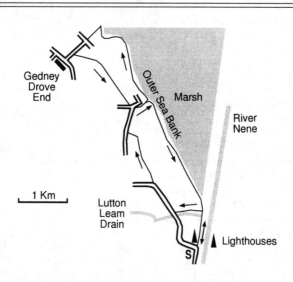

Clearly any 'figure of eight' walk can be split into two. This one is no exception and there is limited parking at the road corner at 479284 near the halfway point. The route described alternates between inland and seaward views for variety. (Do not be tempted to wander out on to the marshes: they are dangerous.)

Take the footpath to the right of the **West Lighthouse** and walk along the river bank. The **East Lighthouse** can be seen on the opposite bank. Cross the sluice of the Lutton Leam and turn inland to reach a road. Turn right and, at a left-hand bend, keep straight on along a track and the top of the **Old Sea Bank**. After about 1,000 yards, steps drop down to a farm track: bear left along this to reach a road and turn right. Go past a footpath sign on the right and, 150 yards further on, bear right along a minor road. At a left-hand corner, walk past a World War II blockhouse and keep ahead to reach the modern sea bank.

Turn left along the bank: when it swings to the left you will see the Wash bombing range ahead. The bank next swings to the right, but before reaching the range buildings you go down some steps, with a handrail, to the left and follow a footpath across a footbridge, heading inland. At a road junction, continue to walk ahead, following a narrow road to reach the old sea bank footpath again, on the left just after a barn. The inns at Gedney Drove End are straight on from here, but the walk turns left.

Follow the old bank path to a road and turn left. (You have walked this short stretch before!) Walk to the top of the outer bank again, but turn right this time. It is now a straightforward walk of $1^1/_4$ miles back to the start by the lighthouse. As you progress you will see **The Artificial Island** and many birds on the **Wash National Nature Reserve**, both to the left. At high tide you can also see shipping heading for the port at Sutton Bridge.

POINTS OF INTEREST:

The West and East Lighthouses – These were built in 1831 to commemorate the completion of the new Nene outfall but were never used as lighthouses. During the 1930s the East Lighthouse (on the far bank) was the home of Sir Peter Scott the artist and naturalist.

Old Sea Bank – This is one of several along this coast. Following the last Ice Age the sea penetrated inland up to 30 miles in places. Since Roman times drainage schemes and sea level changes have allowed the reclamation of large areas of farmland. The biggest reclamations were in the Middle Ages, and again in the 1700s when Dutch engineers built new dykes and straightened local rivers.

The Artificial Island – Almost 2 miles out on the marsh, the island was built in 1975 as ᵣart of a study into freshwater reservoirs. It was designated a Seabird Nesting Reserve in 1987.

The Wash National Nature Reserve – This is the largest National Nature Reserve comprising nearly 10,000 hectares. It is home to a wide range of wildlife and is particularly important in autumn and winter as a feeding ground for ducks, geese and wading birds.

REFRESHMENTS:
The Rising Sun, Gedney Drove End.
The New Inn, Gedney Drove End.

Walk 73   **BIGBY**   7m (11¼km)

Maps: OS Sheets Landranger 112; Pathfinder 719.

Enjoy fabulous views from the Wolds plateau and sleepy villages on the Viking Way.

Start: At 059071, by the telephone box at the bottom of Bigby Hill.

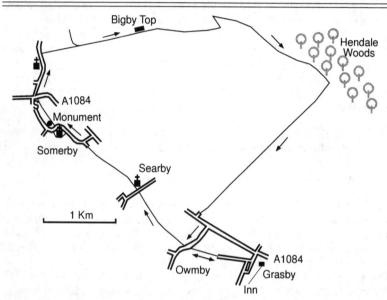

Bigby is on the A1084 east of Brigg. There is limited parking at the start.

Cross the road and walk through Bigby village. Beyond the church and village name sign, look carefully for a footpath sign in the high hedge on the right. The path may be overgrown in summer for the first 50 yards, but then goes up a field, with a hedge to your right, to join a track. Continue forward along this, climbing steadily. Keep forward at a second track junction to pass a barn on **Bigby Top**, with its wonderful views.

At a three-way signpost, turn left and, in 150 yards, turn right along a green lane, ignoring two paths going off to the right. (These paths – Somerby Wold Lane and Searby Wold Lane – provide shorter alternatives without navigational difficulty.)

Walk to the edge of Hendale Wood and, after another 200 yards, take Owmby Wold Lane, signed to the right. This is a good picnic spot. Follow the lane to the A1084, turn left, with care, and then first right down Owmby Hill. As the road bends left, look for the Viking Way signs, by a 1977 Jubilee seat.

(By adding a mile or so you can go left here to Grasby to visit the inn at the crossroads—GR 089050. The Viking Way is excellently waymarked in both directions.)

The route turns right on a clear and well-signed path through fields and woods to **Searby**. Walk down Back Lane, to the left of the church, go around a left-hand bend and cross a footbridge on the right. Go past a pond and continue over a grass field. In the next field, keep to the headland, walking with a hedge on your right. After crossing a footbridge and stile, pass a farmhouse, on your left, and climb a stile on to the farm road. Follow this to the public road and turn left.

Now, when you are level with Somerby church, go through the gate on the left and down the steps into the churchyard. Take the pathway behind the tower to reach a lane, turn right and go right again at a road. A few yards uphill the Viking Way goes off to the left into a grass field to reach the **Somerby Monument**. Continue past this to reach a stile and footbridge. Cross these and one last field to reach Bigby, the telephone box and the start.

POINTS OF INTEREST:

Bigby Top—The views from here alone make the walk worthwhile. To the north-west, Wrawby mill can be clearly seen. It is the only postmill in Lincolnshire, built about 1790. Close by, to the north-east, is Humberside airport, with all its attendant aerial activity, and beyond that is the unusual green copper spire of Kirmington church. In the distance the oil refineries of the Humber Bank are prominent.

Searby – The church here, built in 1832, is of yellow brick, in marked contrast to the stone churches in neighbouring villages. Much of the interior woodwork dates from the 1860s and was made by the vicar. At the corner of Back Lane is a quaint red brick roadside shelter bearing the message *Rest and be thankful*, built by the same vicar.

Somerby Monument—A plaque tells the story of why Edward and Anne Weston built this in 1770 to commemorate their ownership of the Somerby estate for 21 years.

REFRESHMENTS:

There are none on the walk itself, but the suggested detour reaches:
The Cross Keys, Grasby.
There is also plenty of choice in both Caistor or Brigg.

Walk 74   OLD BOLINGBROKE   7¼m (11½km)

Maps: OS Sheets Landranger 122; Pathfinder 783.

An historic castle site and marvellous views.

Start: At 393643, on the wide grass verges just off the A16 north of Toynton-All-Saints.

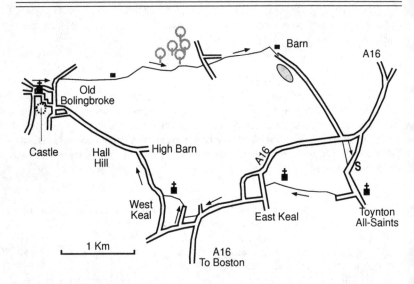

Walk into Toynton-All-Saints and turn right along the lane opposite the church. At the lane end, turn right to follow a farm road down to a stream. Cross a footbridge and continue up the field beyond, with a hedge on your left. Go through a gate and veer slightly right to reach another in the right-hand corner of the next field. Cross a paddock and pass a house to enter a lane. Beyond East Keal Church, where the lane bends right, turn left downhill along a path between houses to reach a road. Bear left, then turn right into Blacksmith Lane and follow it to the A16. Keep ahead along the pavement, then, after about 300 yards, cross, with great care, to the pavement continuation on the other side. Now where the road bends left, just after a minor road joins from the right, go to the right, down a grass bank and climb a fence. Walk along the bottom of the field beyond to reach a stile in the left-hand corner, by a metal barn. Cross, go through a farmyard and then go right, up a lane. Veer left at the top and make the steep climb to **West Keal** church. (The reward is a stunning view over the fens.)

Beyond the church, turn right along a road and follow it over **Hall Hill** and down into **Old Bolingbroke**. On entering the village, keep right when the road forks to reach a T-junction. Go right, and immediately left to reach the castle. After exploring continue along the lane to the inn and church. Bear right, past the church, and walk out of the village, going left along the Mavis Enderby road. After 200 yards, take the uphill path on the right. At the top, go slightly right over an arable field to reach a gate in a wire fence. Go left along a green lane to the site of New America. (NB Near a metal gate the path goes straight on.) At a hedge corner, go over a field to reach another hedge and walk with it on your left. When the hedge bears left, go half-right towards some woods, walking downhill past a footpath sign and going over a stream. Go uphill across rough ground to join a track. Turn left and skirt south of Wheelabout Wood to reach a road. Cross and follow the path opposite: there is a track a few yards to the left which it shortly joins. Keep forward to reach a grey barn near a track junction and a lake. Turn right to reach the A16 again. Cross, with care, and follow the path opposite back to Toynton.

POINTS OF INTEREST:

West Keal – The Wolds end abruptly here with spectacular views from the church porch. Boston and the sea can be seen. Most of the church was built about 1200 but the tower fell in 1881 and was rebuilt.

Hall Hill – From the hill there are fine views towards Old Bolingbroke. Mesolithic flint implements, found here in abundance, indicate an important prehistoric settlement.

Old Bolingbroke – The castle once belonged to John of Gaunt, whose son Henry of Bolingbroke, born here in 1367, became Henry IV. The castle was a Royalist stronghold during the Civil War, but was largely demolished after their defeat at Winceby, 3 miles to the north-west, in 1643. Admission is free and interpretation boards show what it must have looked like in its heyday.

John of Gaunt also built a grand church, but only the south aisle now survives (as the nave) leaving the tower curiously off-set. Look for the stone 'gatepost' near the north-west gate. It is the gravestone of a local carpenter.

REFRESHMENTS:

The Black Horse, Old Bolingbroke.

For a 'cuppa' after the walk there is a mobile transport café in the A16 lay-by north of Toynton (grid reference 396649).

Walk 75   LOUTH AND SOUTH ELKINGTON $7\frac{1}{2}$m (12km)

Maps: OS Sheets Landranger 122; Pathfinder 748.

From market town to countryside and back again.

Start: At 322872, the junction of Westgate and Love Lane in Louth.

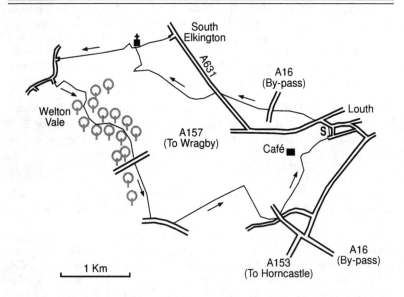

OS Landranger Map 113 (Grimsby) contains 90 per cent of this walk too. Park in Love Lane or in Louth and walk down Westgate to the start.

Walk out of town along Wragby Road and, just after St Mary's Lane, take the school drive on the right. Pass the school and then a farm to reach a stile at the side of a barn. Cross this and the field beyond to reach the bypass. There are stiles on both sides, but please take great care crossing the road. Continue in the same direction to reach some woods. Go through these and down a farm track to a road.

Go straight across, with care, and, in the field opposite, bear half-right to reach a gate on the far side. Go through and turn right to follow a fence and stream to a concrete road. Cross and follow another fence, it is still on your right, for about 400 yards to reach a waymarker and bridlegate – near some rhododendrons. Go through and, after 50 yards, bear sharp right through woods and over a footbridge. At a stile, go half-left up a grass field to reach another stile on the left of **South Elkington** church. Cross on to a farm lane.

Turn left past a pond, then go left again in front of some stables. When the track ends, keep ahead, with a hedge on your left, maintaining direction beyond a stile to reach a farm road at a handgate. Turn right to reach the public road. Go left for 300 yards, and then left again along a track by the sewage works. When you reach the woods, turn right through a valley to reach a road. Cross this with care.

Immediately opposite a permissive path begins: follow it past some trees to reach a footbridge, then bear right to a field corner before heading left, uphill, to reach a road. Turn left and, after 250 yards, turn left again along a clear path over a field, making a bee-line for Louth church spire. Cross a track and continue ahead into a valley. Turn right there and, after going through a gate, turn left. A stile and steps in the far right-hand corner of this field lead down to the road. Go under the by-pass to the entrance to Hubbards Hills.

Walk through the valley and cross the River Lud beyond the café. Go past a house, then through a gate on the left. Now cross Westgate Fields to Love Lane where the walk began.

POINTS OF INTEREST:

This is a walk to enjoy the scenery. Constant variety is provided by fields, woods and valleys near South Elkington and views from the hills when returning to Louth.

South Elkington – The parkland was largely planted in Victorian times when the seeds of some species of trees were first becoming widely available. Specimen trees can be seen here and later in the walk through Welton Vale. Particularly noticeable is Wellingtonia (*Sequoiadendron Giganteum*) from the Sierra Nevada. It grows to a height of 320 ft. Discovered in 1841, and introduced to Britain in 1853 it was named after the Duke of Wellington. In Welton Vale are some Coastal Redwoods, (*Sequoia Sempervirens*), natives of California and Oregon.

There has been a church in the village since the 13th century. Inside is a font from c1400 and unusual painted window frames and columns.

REFRESHMENTS:

On the walk there is only the café in Hubbards Hills, near the end.
The Wheatsheaf Inn, Westgate, Louth is close to the start.
There is a village shop if you detour 250 yards into South Elkington.

Walk 76 **CROWLAND** 7³/₄m (12¹/₂km)

Walk 76 **CROWLAND** $7^3/_4$m ($12^1/_2$km)

Maps: OS Sheets Landranger 131; Pathfinder 878.

Wide fenland skies, the River Welland and the historic town of Crowland.

Start: At 239103, by the triangular Trinity Bridge in Crowland.

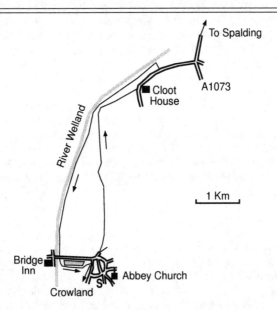

Park in North Street. This easy walk is on short turf virtually the whole way, and is ideal for a brisk spring or autumn day.

From the **Trinity Bridge**, walk up North Street and, at the road junction, take the bridleway ahead on North Bank. After 50 yards, climb the stile on the left and continue along the New River bank top. After the bank veers right it reaches a road at Cloot House.

Walk forward along the road for 500 yards, then turn along a track on the left. This crosses a bridge to reach a pumping station on the **River Welland** bank. (This short section is not a right of way, but the Drainage Board has given permission for its use: please keep off their buildings and equipment.)

Turn left along the bank, keeping a look-out for the many species of birds which live on the river. Follow the bank to reach the B1166 road at a stile. Cross the road to another stile, and turn left beyond it to drop down the bank to a third stile. Cross and walk along on the far side of **The Lake** to reach a wooden footbridge at the far end. Cross and turn right, using the pavement on the top of West Bank and bearing left when West Street is reached. This returns you to the start in the middle of **Crowland**. Walk ahead down East Street to visit **Crowland Abbey**.

POINTS OF INTEREST:

Trinity Bridge – This unique bridge was built in the 13th century where two rivers joined, one of them the Welland. Stand on the top of it to appreciate its site and note the width of North Street and West Street, now with 'islands' of grass, down which the water once flowed. The statue is believed to be Christ holding the world in his hands.

River Welland – Over the centuries the river's course has been much straightened. Early drainage attempts date from before the 1100s, and even in the 1600s efforts were piecemeal and often unsuccessful, though the present course of the river was substantially established then. The surrounding low lying areas were frequently flooded to absorb overflows. Names such as Crowland Wash and Cowbit Wash (further north) recall this. The last major work was as recent as 1954. Watch out for swans, heron and grebe.

The Lake – This is in fact the remains of an old canal, built to link Crowland with the river.

Crowland and Crowland Abbey – There are many old buildings in the town, including several thatched ones. Look out for the cup and saucer in the thatch of the café. The George and Angel is said to be the only inn in the country with this name.

Crowland has been a religious centre since 699 when St Guthlac crossed vast marshes, landed here on an island, and become a hermit. There have been four important abbeys with extensive buildings since then. The present abbey remains, still impressive, and now the parish church, were only a small part of the original. An informative guide and exhibition give a detailed history.

REFRESHMENTS:

The Bridge Inn, Crowland.
The Abbey Hotel, Crowland.
The George and Angel, Crowland.
The Carpenters Arms, Crowland.
The Crown Inn, Crowland.
The Market Café, Crowland.

Walk 77   BURWELL AND LITTLE CAWTHORPE   8m (13km)

Maps: OS Sheets Landranger 122; Pathfinder 748 and (for just a few yards of the route) 766.

Picturesque villages and marvellous views.

Start: At 355796, near the Stags Head Inn, Burwell.

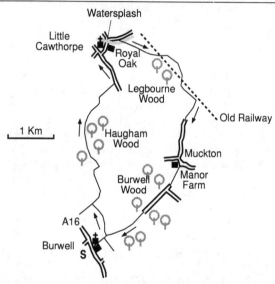

If parking is difficult, then an alternative start point is **Muckton**: see the last paragraph of the route instructions first. Judicious timing might then secure two lots of refreshments!

Walk between the inn and the Buttercross and turn left before the first house, following a path up a field by the church. At the farm track, go left and then keep left at a junction. (You will return by the lane on your right.) At a T-junction go right. The track ends in a field: turn left and head for the right-hand tree of a group of three on the skyline. A waymarker now directs you to the right, along a headland. The headland bears to the left, keeping to the woodland edge to reach another waymarker on a stile. This points into the woods themselves. Go downhill to reach another track which skirts round the edge of the woods again (they are still on your right). Just after bearing sharply right at the woods end, take a downhill track to the left. After about 200 yards, bear left and then, in a few steps, go right to reach a road. Turn left and walk to **Little Cawthorpe**. Turn right down the lane by the church and the pond and cross the footbridge over the watersplash just below the Royal Oak Inn. Follow the path beside the stream, cross another footbridge and take the lane to the right. At the abandoned railway, cross the trackbed and follow the path parallel to it, going through woods on the far side. Where the woods end, re-cross the track to reach a grassy path, still walking parallel to the railway, which is now on your left. After $\frac{1}{2}$ mile turn right and follow a green lane, which is later surfaced, to Muckton.

Turn left and then go right through Manor Farm. Cross a stile in front of the house and go up the grass field beyond. Cross another stile in the top left corner and maintain direction towards the woods ahead. Follow the wide grass path along the edge, crossing a track at a narrow strip of woodland and continuing to reach a second track. Descend a steep valley (just slightly left) and go up the other side. At a gap in the fence (5 yards left of a gas pipeline marker) the farmer's own footpath sign directs you towards **Burwell**. Follow a fieldpath towards a plantation in the shallow valley ahead, soon reaching a grassy track. Go past the plantation and join the main farm track used near the start. Turn left, then right, to return to the start.

POINTS OF INTEREST:

Muckton – The old railway was the Great Northern line to Grimsby. Take time to savour the forlorn atmosphere of the derelict churchyard. Just left of the entrance to Major Farm. The church was demolished in 1983. Note the 'VR' post-box in the Old Rectory gate pillar.

Little Cawthorpe – The red and black church is Victorian, somehow managing to look both incongruous and appealing at the same time. Contrast this with the magnificent Jacobean brickwork of the Manor House, across the road, built in 1673. A pond, vigorous springs, quiet lanes and a delightful watersplash running alongside the inn garden have helped the residents to achieve a 'best kept village' award. There was once a priory here too, near the watersplash.

Burwell – Now little more than a hamlet, straddling the busy A16, Burwell was once even busier. A market charter was granted in the 13th century, one reminder being the octagonal Buttercross, built some 500 years later. On the hillside stands the medieval St Michael's, now redundant. Nearby there was once a Benedictine priory, the only memory being the name of a nearby farm.

REFRESHMENTS:
The Stags Head, Burwell.
The Royal Oak, Little Cawthorpe.

Walk 78   CORBY GLEN AND BURTON-LE-COGGLES   8m (13km)
Maps: OS Sheets Landranger 130; Pathfinder 855 and 856.
Historic villages and unspoilt countryside.
Start: At 999250, Corby Glen Market Place.

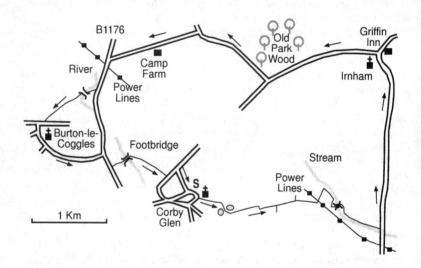

With your back to the Fighting Cocks Inn, leave the Market Place at the far right corner, into Church Street. Walk up to the junction with Morleys Lane. (You could carry on to see the church.) At the footpath sign, enter the farmyard ahead, go through and follow a short lane to a grass field. This is sometimes very muddy, but don't let this 100 yards put you off - the rest of the walk is good underfoot. Go up to a wire fence and turn right along it to reach a stile. Cross, go left at the small pond and then right to reach a second pond. Go to the right of this, keeping the hedge on your left, and, after a few yards, cut left through the hedge and continue forward with the hedge still on your left.

Maintain direction for 1¹/₄ miles - there is a short dog-leg after 400 yards and part of the way is on a green track: do not turn left when the track does. Go under power lines and through a hedge by an old gate. Keep a look-out for deer here. Turn left, walk down to the field corner and turn right to follow a stream. Shortly, cross a footbridge and turn right to reach a road. Turn left and walk to **Irnham**, going left at the junction beyond the entrance to Irnham Hall. In a 'short' mile, after Old Park Wood, turn right along a bridleway. Take the next bridleway on the left - after about $^3/_4$ mile - passing Camp Farm to reach the B1176.

Turn left for 200 yards and then descend steps in the bank on the right to reach a stile. The next few yards can be boggy: aim half-left to reach another stile. Cross the small grass field beyond to reach a footbridge over the river. Cross another stile and walk up a long field with a ditch and hedge on your left. At the top there is a junction of paths above **Burton-le-Coggles**: cross the stile and head towards the church. In the field corner a stile leads on to a road. Go right, then left around the church, following the road to reach the B1176 again.

Turn right, but take the next footpath on the left. Cross a footbridge over the river and bear half-right up a pasture and through a paddock near a large house. Pass a conifer hedge to join a lane on the edge of **Corby Glen**. Go left, and then right to reach the Market Place.

POINTS OF INTEREST:

Irnham – This was Gerneham at the time of Domesday. In the early 1300s the owner of the village was Sir Geoffrey Luttrell and he commissioned a beautiful illustrated psalter (prayer book) depicting a year in the life of the village and its inhabitants. It is now in the British Library. Irnham Hall is an outstanding example of a 16th-century house. The whole village is exceptionally attractive and reminiscent of the Cotswolds.
Burton-le-Coggles – This village was recorded in Domesday as Byrton-en-les-Coggles, presumably because of its cobbled streets. Its charming medieval church is dedicated to St Thomas à Becket.
Corby Glen – This delightful small country town was granted a market charter in 1239 by Henry III. In the Church of St John some 1200 square feet of magnificent medieval wall paintings were discovered in 1939. These are now restored and regarded as the best in Lincolnshire and of national importance. A record which few (if any) other churches can match is that of having only five vicars in 220 years in the period up to 1934. There is a castle motte to the north-west of the church.

REFRESHMENTS:
The Fighting Cocks, Corby Glen.
The Glaziers Arms, Corby Glen.
The Griffin Inn, Irnham.

Walk 79 OSBOURNBY AND NEWTON (VIA HACEBY) 8m (13km)

Maps: OS Sheets Landranger 130; Pathfinder 836.

A quiet walk linking four villages, interesting churches and an ancient salt trading route.

Start: At 069381, Osbournby Market Place.

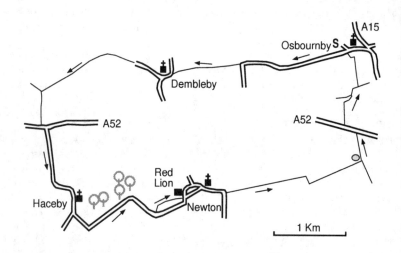

Walk westwards along the road from the far left corner of the Market Place and, where it turns sharp left, go ahead along a green lane to **Dembleby**. Walk a few further yards to the church, then take the lane going half-right just beyond it. After passing a farm, the lane continues as a track, and then a green lane, for 1¼ miles, going gently uphill. Ignore all side tracks, continuing until a T-junction is reached, with footpath signs and waymarks. Turn left, but after a few paces turn sharp right, and then left again and walk down to the main A52 road.

Cross this, with care, and follow the lane slightly to your left. (**Warning** – This road is busy and a bend reduces visibility. Walking a short way to the right for a better view, and returning along the other side, is strongly recommended.) Follow the lane through **Haceby**, going left at a T-junction for **Newton**. After a sharp right-hand bend, take the second signed footpath to the left. This follows a stream to a footbridge. Cross and continue following the stream to reach a road in Newton, near the Red Lion Inn.

Newton is built around an oval, so either take the lane opposite, or the one just beyond the inn. Both lanes lead round to the church. Now go along the Walcot road and, where this bends right, continue along the track ahead. Go around a double bend and, further on, through a metal gate, then go left over a stile just beyond a pond. Go down a headland to reach another stile. Cross and turn left to walk along the verge of the **A52**, taking great care.

After 100 yards, cross, with even greater care, and go down the headland path opposite, with a hedge on your right. Cross the stile near the bottom of the field, then bear half-left to go through a hedge gap. Continue to reach another stile, on your left, and cross to join a green lane. Go right to reach a bridge on the left, just beyond a seat. Cross and, after 200 yards, move left so that the hedge is now on your right. At the top of the field bear left for just a few steps and then watch closely for a narrow path on the right, (before the farm buildings). Take this path, following it back to **Osbournby** Market Place.

POINTS OF INTEREST:

Dembleby – The church has an unusual dedication to St Lucia, a Sicilian lady martyred after torture about the year 303AD. Though only built in 1867 the church incorporates the Norman arch from an earlier building.

Haceby – This must once have been a bigger village to justify its beautiful church. Parts of the tower and chancel are Norman, but the building is now redundant.

Newton – Roman occupation is known throughout the Sleaford area and the village lies half-way between two Roman roads – King Street to the west and Mareham Lane to the east. A Roman villa was discovered in 1818 at grid reference 019369 near to where the walk crosses the A52. It was excavated in 1929 but is now covered again. St Botolph's Church is possibly so named because of connections with a monastery founded by the saint in the 7th century at Boston 20 miles away.

A52 – The main road largely follows the Salters Way, an ancient trade highway from the salt marshes around the Wash to the Midlands, crossing the River Witham just south of Grantham.

Osbournby – Note the old houses spread around the Market Place. Years ago this was a village green. The church is worth a visit to view its carved benches.

REFRESHMENTS:
The Whichcote Arms, Osbournby, just off route on the A15.
The Red Lion, Newton.

Walk 80   THE HUMBER BRIDGE   8m (13km)

Maps: OS Sheets Landranger 112 or 106; Pathfinder 696.

A Nature Reserve by the Humber, then over the suspension bridge.

Start: At 028234, the bridge viewpoint and picnic site.

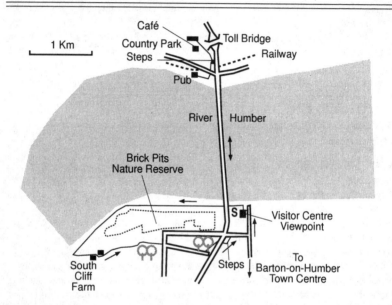

The viewpoint/picnic site is signed from Barton-on-Humber. There is no bridge toll for pedestrians.

Walk to the river bank by the Visitor Centre and turn left. Follow the path under the bridge passing one of the few remaining tile works. Continue for about a mile to reach two metal gates with adjacent kissing gates. (Various paths on the **Barton Clay Pits Nature Reserve** can be explored if desired: there is a second Visitor Centre at the far end of the Reserve.) Go through both gates and continue along the bank, reaching a footpath sign beyond a white navigation beacon. Descend to the left, cross a footbridge and bear left along the field edge to South Cliff Farm. Go behind some barns and then turn right (waymarkers on the wall), before turning left along a track across the front of the farmhouse. Where the main track branches left, a stile is partly concealed just to the left in the high hedge ahead. Go over and cross a field to a small wood. Bear left for a few yards, then go right over a footbridge. Resume your original direction in the next field to reach a stile at a road junction. Walk down the lane opposite and, at the end, go left through a handgate on to a signed path through woodland. The path emerges opposite the pedestrian access to the **Humber Bridge**.

Walk up the steps and over the bridge. The views are spectacular as large ships pass beneath your feet. At the far side steps on the left lead down into the Country Park car park. (To the left of the cafeteria another path provides a short walk under a railway and a road to reach the water's edge, an old mill and an inn.) Return over the bridge: there are two walkways so you could go beneath it to climb up and return along the other side. Descend the steps on the south bank and turn along the pavement towards Barton. Just before the first houses, turn left along a footpath beside a hedge to return to the start.

POINTS OF INTEREST:

Barton Clay Pits Nature Reserve – Brick and tile making was once a major industry here. The local clay is now largely used up and only a few yards still exist. One of these, Wm Blyths, is passed on the walk. The worked out pits are now flooded and have become a huge Nature Reserve, home to a wide variety of wild life habitats.

The Humber Bridge – This triumph of British engineering took eight years to build. Begun in 1972 it was opened by the Queen in 1981. A few mind boggling statistics are: Span between towers – 4,626 ft (San Fransisco's Golden Gate is 4,200 ft); Total Length – 7,284 ft; Wire used – 44,000 miles; Cable weight – 10,826 tons; Concrete used – 472,416 tons; Weight of road deck – 16,239 tons. The bridge was made in 124 pieces, each separately floated in and lifted into position.

About 5 miles upstream there was a Roman ferry at the end of Ermine Street. For centuries any crossing was a lengthy and hazardous undertaking. Even when the railway companies established a ferry at New Holland, cars had to negotiate slippery planks or be man-handled aboard.

REFRESHMENTS:

On the north bank there is a cafeteria in the Country Park car park and *The Country Park Inn* and a café are by the water's edge.

The Westfield Lakes Hotel is passed on the walk.

There are also numerous possibilities in Barton-on-Humber. The nearest to the start of the walk are:

The Sloop, Waterside Road.

The White Swan, near the station.

Walk 81   **TEALBY AND KIRMOND-LE-MIRE**   8m (13km)
Maps: OS Sheets Landranger 113; Pathfinders 730 and 747.
A varied walk over the Wolds.
Start: At 156905, the King's Head Inn.

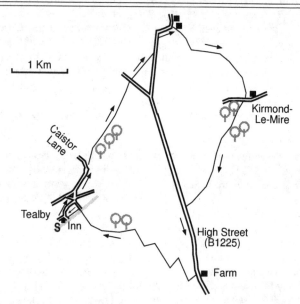

Parking is with the landlords permission: please seek it, and show consideration for other patrons. The walk is on good paths, tracks or roads, with the exception of one large arable field after Kirmond-le-Mire.

Turn left from the inn car park, walking uphill through **Tealby** via Front Street. Go left up Beck Hill and cross the B1203 near the church. Continue up Caistor Lane and, at a sharp left-hand bend, take the track ahead, uphill, past woods. At the far corner of these, go straight on over an arable field to reach a stile. Cross and go down a grass field to another stile. Cross and keep ahead by a waymarker, aiming for a clump of beech trees by a road. Cross the road and continue along a fieldpath to reach a minor road.

Turn left and, at a left-hand bend, before a farm, take the footpath through the hedge on the right. Go past a cottage and follow the path to a field corner. Go uphill

152

through trees, and then slightly left. Cross a footbridge and follow a narrow grass path over a large field. Go through two gates and follow a track to Manor Farm at **Kirmond-le-Mire**. Walk past the farmhouse to the road, noting the pun on the farm name on a board advertising produce for sale.

Do not take the bridleway immediately opposite: instead, go right, up the road, for 80 yards, then turn left at another bridleway signpost. Bear right around some woods, on your right, and follow the edge of the field for some 200 yards. There is no waymarker here, but near some conifers go left to cross the field. On the far side there are more woods and, to their right, a large single tree. To the right of that is a handgate in a wire fence. Go through and turn right before veering left up a shallow, grassy valley. Beyond the gate at the top, turn right along a track to the High Street (the B1225).

Turn left and, using the wide grass verges, follow the road for about $^3/_4$ mile before turning right, opposite High Street Farm, along the Viking Way. This National Trail is well-waymarked as it zig-zags down to Tealby. After three 'rights' and two 'lefts' it joins a farm track: turn left, passing the site of **Bayons Manor** to reach a ford and footbridge. Cross and turn left immediately along a path that returns to the start.

POINTS OF INTEREST:

Tealby – Long regarded as one of Lincolnshire's prettiest villages, Tealby nestles on the western Wolds' slopes. Because of its good water supply there is a long history of settlement. Mentioned in the Domesday book as *Tavelsbi*, it had then a population of 250 with fourteen watermills in the vicinity. The church, standing sentinel more like a castle on its hilltop, has stonework going back to the Normans.

Kirmond-le-Mire – This area was settled in prehistoric times. The High Street was a Roman road and on the hillside to the east of the manor there are lynchets – ancient farming terraces – which may have been an early vineyard. The village lies in a steep sided hollow, the name a comment on the original state of the roads hereabouts, though the *Kirmond* part comes from the French *Chevre mont*, meaning *Goat Hill*.

Bayons Manor – This once belonged to Odo, a brother of the Conqueror, and Bishop of Bayeux. The last Manor House was built in 1836-42 by Charles Tennyson D'Eyncourt, uncle to the poet Alfred Lord Tennyson. Designed as an extravagant Gothic castle, it was complete with towers, moat and drawbridge. It is no more, having been blown up in the early 1960s, because of its derelict state.

REFRESHMENTS:

The Kings Head, Tealby, (dating from 1357 this is a rare example of a thatched pub). There is a tea-room in Front Street.

Walk 82   THE LOUTH CANAL AND ALVINGHAM   8m (13km)

Maps: OS Sheets Landranger 113; Pathfinders 731 and 748.

Birdlife and industrial archaeology on the canal and a working pottery and watermill at Alvingham.

Start: At 338881, Riverhead, Louth.

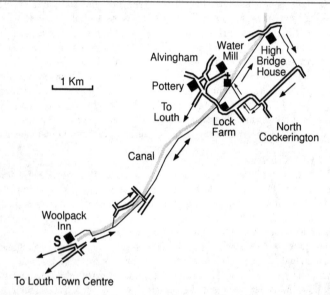

Flat it may be, but on a bright sunny day the 'marsh' has a fascination all its own. This walk is of interest to both naturalist and historian.

From Louth town centre follow Eastgate and Ramsgate to Riverhead Road, turning off by the Woolpack Inn and parking 150 yards further on.

A direct return from Alvingham, omitting the North Cockerington loop, saves 3 miles (5km).

Walk away from the town to cross the **Louth Canal** at the first footbridge. Continue beside the canal until you can re-cross it at another footbridge. Now go across a field and turn right along the lane on the far side. At a T-junction, cross the canal for a third time and follow its bank for 1¹/₂ miles to reach the road at Lock Farm, Alvingham. Turn left along the road, going left again at a junction, then right into Yarburgh Road. Walk around **Alvingham** by turning right after the pottery, right again into Highbridge Road and then left into Church Lane. Pass the watermill and go through a farm into the churchyard and the **Two Churches**. Cross the bridge in the right-hand corner, going over the canal again.

Turn left and walk to High Bridge House. Cross a stile and go right along the 'No Through Road' until the tarmac ends. There, turn right along a bridleway. Bear left near a white house and continue to reach another road. Turn right to North Cockerington, ignoring a road on the left. After a right-hand bend, take the footpath on the left, crossing the lawn of Ringwells Farm to reach a stile into a small pasture. From the other side of the pasture a second stile leads to a path beside a fence. Follow the path over two further stiles to meet a hedged path at right angles. Turn right, go over a road and walk to the canal. Turn left and follow the canal back to Louth.

POINTS OF INTEREST:

The Louth Canal – Of the 7 locks on the canal, 6 were between Alvingham and Louth. The first vessel used the canal in 1770 and despite competition from the railways canal traffic lasted over 150 years until 1924. The locks remain in remarkably good condition. Still carrying the waters of the River Lud to the sea, the canal and its banks now support many species of plants, flowers and birds.

Alvingham – The village is built around a rectangle of roads and still retains many old farm buildings. The pottery is open daily to visitors. In Highbridge Road there is an old Methodist Chapel, built in 1836, and the stocks still stand at the corner of Church Lane. The picturesque watermill is 17th-century. It too opens to the public, but only on certain days in July and August.

The Two Churches – Two churches sharing one churchyard, a most unusual situation. St Mary's (the nearest to Alvingham) was in fact the parish church of North Cockerington! Originating as a chapel for a nearby Gilbertine priory, it became redundant in 1981. Alvingham's church is dedicated to St Adelwold. Some priory earthworks (probably fishponds) can be seen by the canal.

REFRESHMENTS:

The Woolpack, Louth, is closest to the start, but there are numerous other possibilities in the town.

Walk 83   SWAYFIELD AND CASTLE BYTHAM   8m (13km)

Maps: OS Sheets Landranger 130; Pathfinders 855, 856, 876 and 877.

A cross country route to an ancient castle site.

Start: At 992228, the Royal Oak Inn, Swayfield.

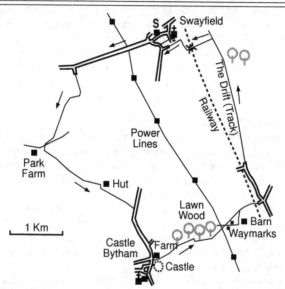

Two sections of this walk, one not waymarked, traverse arable fields. Careful navigation is required to reach Park Farm. Parking at the inn is with the landlord's permission.

From the inn, turn right. Walk along High Street, then follow Overgate Road and, at a Water Authority compound, turn left along an unsigned track. Where this ends, walk ahead past telegraph poles to reach a ditch at the field bottom. Turn right to the field corner, where the ditch comes down from your right in a wide curve. Cross – you will have to jump! – and turn left to pass through a hedge gap. Walk uphill towards a group of trees on the skyline. Behind these, continue beside a ditch, heading downhill to join a farm track. Turn right to reach Park Farm. Turn left by the first buildings (waymarkers begin here) walking downhill to another track. Turn left along this for 500 yards, then watch for a waymarker directing you through the hedge to your right. On the opposite side, at the field corner, go down right to another track, following this past a black hut to a road. Turn right into **Castle Bytham**. Turn right into Water Lane, passing the village pump, to reach a footpath signed on the left. At the top of the paddock, bear left between cottages and then walk up Pinfold Road. Turn left and, beyond the Castle Inn, bear left down Castlegate.

At the entrance to Castle Farm, on the right, cross the footbridge before going left to reach a stile in a hedge. Walk up the next field to join a wire fence leading to another stile at the top corner. Cross and turn left to pass Lawn Wood. At the woods' end there is a ditch: look for a concealed waymarker in the undergrowth on your left. Go into the adjacent field. The right of way is to the right of an electricity pylon. Aim between a ruined barn and a copse seen on the horizon. Following waymarkers you will cross a track and rejoin it later, lower down, on the far side of the hill. (A rough track does go along by the woods to join this main one, which if followed passes the barn.) Go under the railway to reach a road at Creeton. Turn left, but when the road bends left, go ahead along a wide track. After $1^1/_4$ miles there is a pronounced hollow. At the far side, on the left, is a footpath for Swayfield: go under the railway, bearing half-right at a waymarker on the other side. Cross a field to a fence corner and climb the stile by a drinking trough. Turn right, passing Church Farm via a gate and a cattle-grid. Walk to a road and turn right towards **Swayfield**. Just before a bend take the path to the right to reach a kissing-gate at the churchyard. Turn left up the lane past the Armada Beacon and then left again to regain the start.

POINTS OF INTEREST:

Castle Bytham – Pond, stream, village pump, inn and castle - Castle Bytham has all the attributes of a typical English village. The castle site dominates, though only the defensive mound now remains. Belonging to Earl Morcar in Saxon times, a large Norman castle was built after the Conquest by Drogo, brother-in-law of William the Conqueror. It was destroyed by fire during the Wars of the Roses.

Swayfield – The church here is well away from the present village, the earlier surrounding houses having been burned down to restrict plague infection in the 17th century. There was an Armada beacon here in 1588, the modern replica was erected in 1988. The main east coast railway line passes the village at its highest point between London and Scotland.

REFRESHMENTS:

The Royal Oak, Swayfield. (Oliver Cromwell is reputed to have lodged here.)
The Castle Inn, Castle Bytham.

Walk 84   BARNOLDBY-LE-BECK AND RAVENDALE   8m (13km)

Maps: OS Sheets Landranger 113; Pathfinders 720 and 731.
Attractive villages, fields, streams and valleys.
Start: At 236032, in Barnoldby-le-Beck.

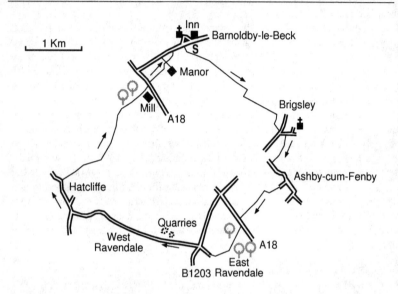

Park by the telephone box opposite Church Lane. The Ship Inn car park may be used if you first seek the landlord's permission. The inn is halfway round if you park in West Ravendale and adapt the route instructions.

From the phone box, go through a kissing gate and follow a path that goes slightly left, then veers right to continue as a clear path to join a farm track. Turn right for 70 yards and then left (no waymarker) along a field edge. At a corner the path narrows, entering undergrowth and aiming for Brigsley Church, seen ahead. After a short dog-leg over stiles it reaches the road in Brigsley next to a shop selling homemade ice-cream. Cross into Waithe Lane. Now look for a path on the right opposite a thatched cottage. Cross a footbridge and keep ahead across a grass field to reach a lane. Turn left to **Ashby-cum-Fenby**. In the village, turn right into Post Office Lane. At the end, by a fieldgate, there is a stile: cross and veer right to another stile, then cross a field diagonally to reach a white gate. Go through and walk with a hedge on your right to the next field corner where there is a concealed stile. Cross and turn right to go through a gap in a hedge ahead. Turn left along a wide grass path, going uphill to reach the A18, formerly the B1431. Turn left, then after 50 yards, cross, with care, to turn right along a bridleway. Go uphill, through a metal gate, and keep ahead through some woods until you can bear right just beyond, walking parallel with the drive to a house. The path curves past some conifers to join a gravel road at a signpost. Turn right, downhill, through **East Ravendale** to reach the B1203 Binbrook road.

Continue along the quiet road opposite, through **West Ravendale**, for about $1\frac{1}{2}$ miles. At a road junction, after the second cattle-grid, turn right into Hatcliffe. Ignore the road signed to Barnoldby, walking through Hatcliffe to reach the hill out of the village. Take the path on the right just after the last bungalow, keeping below a children's playground to reach a stile near a Water Board building. Cross and walk beside a stream, at first on a grass track and then a grass path, following the stream through fields and woods, and past mill buildings to reach the A18 again. Cross, again with care, and follow the path opposite beside a metal fence. Continue along a headland until you are level with the Manor House. Here, waymarkers direct you left along the access road for 50 yards, then right over a stile. Cross a meadow behind a large house to reach a stile in the fence on your left. Cross and follow the path beyond over a footbridge to a road. Turn right back to **Barnoldby-le-Beck**.

POINTS OF INTEREST:

Ashby-cum-Fenby – The church is just off route down the lane to Hall Farm. It stands next to almshouses founded in 1641.

East Ravendale – A Lincolnshire architect, James Fowler, designed and built the church in 1857. Although there are steps to the pulpit now, a small door behind it was once the only access. There is some high quality Victorian stained glass and a charming framed water colour by Fowler of the church and school next door which he also designed. The village letterbox is set into the school wall.

Ravendale – A local beauty spot. This lovely wooded valley has old chalk quarries by the roadside. Priory Farm marks the site of a 13th-century priory.

Barnoldby-le-Beck – A detour along Church Lane leads to an unusual obelisk in memory of William Smith, huntsman to the Earl of Yarborough, who fell from his horse and died on 11th April 1885.

REFRESHMENTS:
The Ship Inn, Barnoldby-le-Beck.

Walk 85   **WARTER**   8m (13km)

Maps: OS Sheets Landranger 106; Pathfinder 666 and 675.

Good tracks, mostly grass, with some moderate hills near the start and finish. A little exposed in poor weather.

Start: At 872504, a small lay-by next to the village pond in Warter.

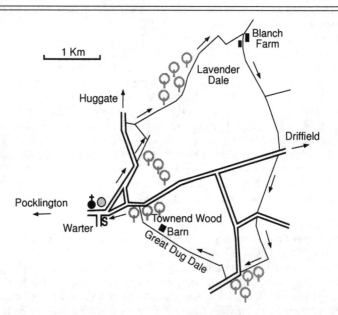

From the pond, walk up the Huggate road, ascending steadily. As the gradient eases at a left-hand bend, take the grass track straight ahead. The track turns left before reaching a junction: turn sharp right and follow the track around the edge of a plantation. Beyond the plantation the track narrows, and passes between a hedge and a fence, descending through a small gate into the open Lavender Dale. Cross and ascend the opposite side of the Dale, then turn left along the clear track which steadily climbs to reach a line of trees. The path ahead is less clear, so walk just below the tree line to reach a small gate. Go through and keep high, soon joining a track rising from below. Follow the track rightwards, go through a gate and, shortly, bear left to reach **Blanch Farm**.

Turn right in front of the farmhouse, going along the wide concrete track. This section of the route is part of the waymarked Minster Way. The Way departs at a junction, to the left, where you continue ahead, going along a now rough track to reach the B1246. Cross the road, with care, and walk along a good grass track with a hedge on your left. This track crosses Middleton Road before reaching a narrow plantation. Continue along the track as it turns right in front of the plantation to reach a minor road at a sharp corner. Walk ahead, along the road, soon reaching the end of the field on your right. There, turn along a path, with a hedge and fence to your left. Follow the headland path as it turns left and then bears right, going along the rim of Great Dugdale.

Pass to the left of a small barn, crossing a stile, and continue to walk with a fence on your left as you gradually descend to Townend Wood. A narrow, but clear, path winds down through the wood: at its end, cross a stile and turn left, with care, along the B1246. Follow the road for the short distance back to the start in **Warter**.

POINTS OF INTEREST:

Warter – The village is worth visiting for the imposing St James' Church and, alongside a small green, the lovely row of thatched cottages.

Blanch Farm – Walkers will be pleased to know that the barking sheepdogs are safely housed in kennels by the side of this very isolated white farmhouse.

REFRESHMENTS:

Warter is 'dry', but it is only 3 miles to Huggate and the Wold Inn, or 4 miles to Pocklington where there is a good choice.

Walk 86   BARMBY ON THE MARSH   8m (13km)

Maps: OS Sheets Landranger 106; Pathfinder 694 and 685.
Very flat walking along riverbank and field paths.
Start: At 681286, the NRA car park at Derwent Barrage.

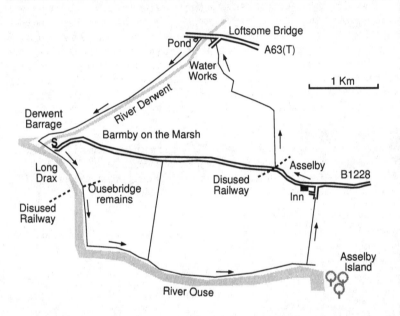

From the **Derwent Barrage** car park, walk towards the **River Derwent**, but quickly turn left and cross a stile which gives access to the **River Ouse** embankment. The first few miles of the route follows the winding river bank: go past the remains of the railway bridge and, soon after a sharper bend, go through gates at the end of a track which provides a short cut back to Barmby. Now continue for some distance to reach a second set of gates. There, turn left and follow the track (Landing Lane) to the village of **Asselby**.

Continue straight ahead, past some houses, to reach Main Street. Turn left along the footpath by the side of this fairly quiet road, passing, or pausing at, the Black Swan Inn. At the western end of the village, and shortly after a double bend in the road and opposite a farm building, turn right along a track.

A few signs remain here of a disused railway, but the route does not follow this. Instead, it goes past a junction of drains on the left, and keeps ahead where a track leaves to the right. The track soon bears left: follow the path diversion along this as it becomes rougher to reach the corner of a water works and a line of electricity pylons. Turn right, with the hedge on your left, then turn left again at the next corner to follow the field headland, with a hedge – for most of the way – on your right. Reach and cross the access road to the water works, and then go over a stile. Turn right and walk to Loftsome Bridge, which carries the A63(T) over the River Derwent.

Cross the bridge, with care, and, soon, cross the stile on the left to reach the western bank of the river. Walk along the embankment, passing a small, reed-filled pond on your right, and the water works on the opposite bank. The tall steeple of Hemingborough church is clear on the right, while ahead, Drax Power Station looms large.

Cross a stile to re-enter the amenity area by the Derwent Barrage. A picnic site is followed by fencing which shields a pond area: you may wish to spend a little time in the hide to view wildfowl on the pond. Finally, note the lock and the arrangements made for small boats as you cross the Barrage and return to the car park.

POINTS OF INTEREST:

Derwent Barrage – The Barrage, in the care of the National Rivers Authority, was constructed to prevent flooding by tidal surges up the River Ouse. It also keeps the Derwent as a fresh water river, and the water works extracts water for use over a wide area. The site has been developed as an amenity area, with car park, toilets, picnic areas, and a pond area for wildfowl.

River Derwent – The river is navigable up to Sutton upon Derwent, though attempts have been made to re-open locks up to Malton.

River Ouse – The river carries its share of small craft, including some from York.

Asselby – The village has some interesting gardens to view as you pass through. Note the statues in a garden reached shortly before Main Street.

REFRESHMENTS:
The King's Head Inn, Barmby.
The Black Swan Inn, Asselby.

Walk 87   **PATRINGTON**   8m (13km)

Maps: OS Sheets Landranger 113; Pathfinder 697 and 708.

Gentle walking along field paths, tracks and quiet roads.

Start: At 316226, St Patrick's Church, Patrington.

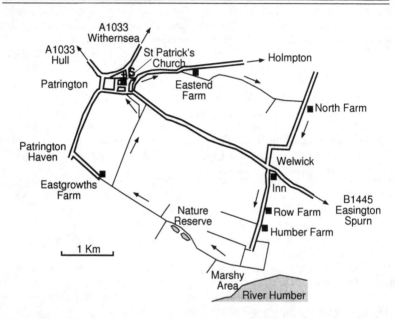

From **St Patrick's Church**, walk eastwards to reach a road junction. Turn left along Holmpton Road and, at a left-hand bend, just before a seat with an unusual wooden arch behind it, take the footpath on the right. Follow the path across a field to reach the right-hand side of Eastend Farm. Now continue ahead along a grass path which goes between crops and then to the right of a small drain. Turn left at the drain corner. The field narrows: turn right to cross at the narrowest point, heading towards a gap in the hedge. Here, another hedge continues ahead with a, now grass, path on its left.

Cross a farm track and continue to reach some wartime buildings. Here, follow an access road to reach Northfield Lane close to North Farm. Turn right and follow this quiet lane into Welwick. To explore the village, turn right along Main Street to reach **St Mary's Church**, passing a home-made bakery shop.

Return along the street, passing the Coach and Horses Inn, and turn right down Humber Lane. This becomes Row Lane: follow the wider lane as it turns sharp right at a junction, where a narrower track goes ahead. Soon, turn left along a second narrow track, following it to reach the River Humber embankment by an area of Saltmarsh. Turn right, along the embankment.

Where the embankment turns sharp left, to the north of a wide drain, descend and continue along a narrow path which follows an uncultivated area of bushes between fields. This marks the start of the **Haverfield Quarries Nature Reserve**: the path is permissive. The path becomes a wider track and passes two large ponds: you may pause to observe the wildlife from the hide between the ponds. Now keep to the main track ahead and go through a gate at the end of the reserve. Beyond, a bridleway goes ahead, towards Eastgrowths Farm. Before reaching the farm, turn right along a rough wide track (Saltmarsh Lane). The lane improves before reaching the B1445 (Welwick road). Turn left, back into Patrington, and, as the road bends, turn left along Southgate. Now take the first lane on the right to return to the church.

POINTS OF INTEREST:

St Patrick's Church, Patrington – This is a beautiful building, worthily called the Queen of Holderness.

St Mary's Church, Welwick – This is an interesting village church. A collection of old farm machinery may be on display next door.

Haverfield Quarries Nature Reserve – The Reserve is a narrow length of bushes and ponds between fields and supports a good variety of wildlife.

REFRESHMENTS:

The Holderness Inn, Patrington.

The Coach and Horses Inn, Welwick.

The small home bakery near the church at Welwick is very tempting!

Walk 88   INGHAM TO GLENTWORTH $8^3/_4$m (14km)

Maps: OS Sheets Landranger 121; Pathfinder 746.

Explore the countryside below the Lincoln 'cliff': good tracks and paths link three pretty villages.

Start: At 946835, on the village green, Ingham.

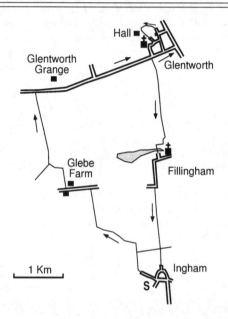

Leave **Ingham** down the 'No Through Road' past the Post Office and turn right into Short Lane. At a bridleway sign, walk forward 10 yards to another sign and turn left by a dyke. Follow this to the far corner of the field and turn right there to cross two sleeper bridges. Now follow a grass track to a road. Turn left, walk past two farms and take the next bridleway on the right, following it along the field edge to a corner. There, go left to reach a footbridge, being careful of your ankles in the rabbit burrows. Cross the bridge and go half-left over the field beyond to reach a bridleway sign about 100 yards away. Take the track on the right to reach a road. Turn right and walk into Glentworth. The bridleway on the right near the first road junction is the return route. But first make a tour of **Glentworth** village.

Keep ahead to the next junction. Turn left, pass Stoney Lane and walk to the bottom of St George's Hill. Round the corner and go left into Hillside Road. At its end there is a stile and signpost: go diagonally left across the field beyond to the far corner. Cross a ditch and walk up to a track and the pillars of the Hall gateway. Turn left, go past Glentworth Hall and walk back into the village. Go right, passing the church and continuing to the road junction and the bridleway passed earlier.

Follow the bridleway, at first along a track and then across two fields with a hedge on your left to meet another track. Continue along this until just before a green barn. There at the waymarkers, go right, then left to reach a handgate. Go through and turn right beside a fence to reach another handgate. **Fillingham Castle** can be seen on the hillside as you cross the bridge ahead, over the lake, and walk to the main street.

Turn left to **Fillingham Church,** then return and walk through the village. Bear left, go past the Post Office and, after a little over $^1/_4$ mile, at a right-hand bend, keep ahead along a track. When this bends left, go forward over the footbridge ahead and cross a field towards a large house. (You will lose sight of it briefly.) At a track and another footbridge, cross a final field, this time aiming just right of the house. A tree-lined lane leads into Ingham: turn right to return to the green.

POINTS OF INTEREST:

Ingham – The older part of the village clusters around the green at the bottom of the hill. The old school has an unusual open-sided tower. During World War II the Black Horse Inn was a favourite with the *Dambusters* from nearby RAF Scampton.

Glentworth – The church has a striking monument to Sir Christopher Wray (1524-1592), an eminent judge during the reign of Queen Elizabeth I. He built the Hall at Glentworth, but only a fragment of his building remains in the present one. This was built in 1753, but is itself now a ruin.

Fillingham Castle – This was built in the 1760s, strategically sited with its view over the church, village and lake. The bridge was restored for the 1995 VE Day celebrations, with new parapets to the original design.

Fillingham Church – John Wycliffe (1329-1384), the religious reformer, was rector here from 1361 to 1368. He made the first complete translation of the Bible into English. The unusual tower has open-sided arches on three sides.

REFRESHMENTS:
The Black Horse, Ingham.
The Inn on the Green, Ingham.

Walk 89   **CAYTHORPE AND CARLTON SCOOP**   9m (14¹/₂km)

Maps: OS Sheets Landranger 130; Pathfinder 814.

A fairly demanding walk on hills and heathland.

Start: At 939485, Caythorpe church.

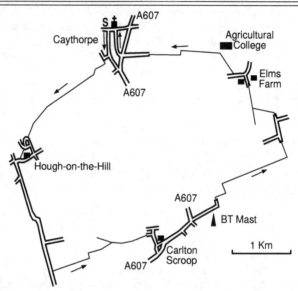

From the church, walk down High Street and turn right into South Parade. At the corner, turn left and immediately right along a path beside a hedge. Follow the path to a stile with a five-way footpath signpost. Cross and turn right towards **Hough-on-the-Hill** visible 1¹/₄ miles away. Follow a hedge/fence, cross a track, and then walk beside a dyke. On reaching a grass field, bear slightly left to reach a stile in the far corner. Walk along the lane opposite and, at a junction, take the rising footpath (by the railings) just to your right. Walk uphill, then turn right to go through the churchyard into the village. Turn left by the Brownlow Arms, leaving Hough along the Grantham road. Follow the road for almost 1¹/₄ miles, ignoring the first signed footpath on the left, but taking the second, the Viking Way, about 300 yards further on. The path is well waymarked: stay on it to the edge of Carlton Scroop where it joins a track just before reaching a road.

Turn right along the road, then left, passing Carlton Scroop church to reach the A607. Turn left along the road, with care, following it to a distinct left bend. There, cross, with great care, and go up Heath Lane. Beyond the BT mast the lane bends left: keep ahead when it doubles back as a farm track. After three turns in quick succession (right, left and right again) the path ascends to open heath. Walk to the junction with **Pottergate** (at GR 969464, recognised by its fourway fingerpost) and turn left. You will soon join a metalled road: walk ahead along this, but go straight ahead when it bends right. Then, almost at once, bear half-left at a fingerpost to head towards another fingerpost visible on the far side of a large field. There, join a track going to the right and walk through Elms Farm, part of the Agricultural College, to reach a road. Turn left, then, beyond the college buildings, right along a footpath. Follow the path over stiles and across several paddocks, gradually going slightly leftwards and downhill. At a waymarker, stay below a long shed, beyond which bear left, downhill, with a hedge on your left. When you reach a stile, ensure that your continued descent is still with the hedge to your left. At a plank bridge go left through a thicket, then turn right. Now keep forward across a field and through gates on to Love Lane, continuing to reach the A607. Cross, with care, and follow Old Lincoln Road into **Caythorpe**. At the T-junction you will then see the church to your left.

POINTS OF INTEREST:

Hough-on-the-Hill – The church is famous for its semi-circular Saxon tower staircase of which there are only three others in the country. In the porch, carved on the stone seats, are medieval equivalents of our modern board games. There is an Anglo-Saxon cemetery, where over 2,000 burials have been excavated, on nearby Loveden Hill. By the church there is a motte and bailey site. The inn, school and other old stone houses combine to make this a most attractive village.

Pottergate – This was part of an ancient route on the belt of Jurassic rocks stretching up the country from the south-west and known to archaeologists as *The Jurassic Way*.

Caythorpe – The outside of the church is 'striped' limestone and ironstone. The spire is impressive at 156 feet (45 metres), although it was 10 feet higher before the rebuilding that followed a lightning strike in 1859. Inside it is unique in Lincolnshire, at least as a medieval church. The nave has a central division of pillars and arches rising to the roof ridge. Around the church there are many old houses, especially in Church Lane. The oak tree at the church gate was planted to commemorate the 60th year of Queen Victoria's reign.

REFRESHMENTS:

The Red Lion, Caythorpe.
The Eight Bells, Caythorpe.
The Brownlow Arms, Hough-on-the-Hill.

Walk 90   BURTON AGNES AND RUDSTON   9m (14½km)

Maps: OS Sheets Landranger 101; Pathfinder 657.

Fairly easy walking, with two gentle climbs, in an historic area.

Start: At 104630, the southern end of the pond in Burton Agnes.

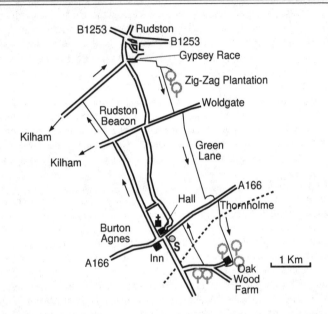

Turn left, with care, along the A166 in **Burton Agnes**. Cross and turn right, along the Rudston Road, with **Rudston Roam** waymarkers guiding you. At a junction, keep ahead on the narrower road which steadily rises to **Woldgate**. Turn left at the T-junction and, soon, turn right, along a bridleway, walking with a hedge on your left. The bridleway descends to the Kilham to Rudston road: turn right to reach **Rudston**.

Turn left, and then right, down Eastgate. Ignore a footpath sign, continuing to reach the bridge over the Gypsey Race stream. Cross the bridge and immediately turn left. When you reach a T-junction, turn right to reach the church, then take the road going downhill on the right. Go right again at the bottom, cross the bridge again and turn left at the footpath sign. Follow the path over stiles and through a farmyard to reach a track. Turn left along the track. Soon after a sharp right-hand bend, the track bears left below Zig-Zag Plantation. Here, leave the main track, and the Rudston Roam, and turn right, up a bridleway, with the plantation on your left.

Follow the bridleway to Woldgate. Turn left and, soon, right, down a green lane, following it to reach the A166 at Thornholme. Turn left, with care, go past bungalows on the right, and then cross, with even greater care, to reach a large gate. Go through and follow the footpath across an open field, aiming for the right-hand corner. Before the corner is reached, follow a hedge, crossing several stiles and then carefully following the track over the railway line. Continue along the track which follows the side of Demming Drain until the drain bears left. A hedge separates the fields here: take the left-hand field and continue in a southerly direction with a hedge on your right. Eventually you will reach a small plantation: keep ahead and cross a track, with Oak Wood Farm on your right.

Follow the edge of the trees to the south of the farm to reach the farm access road. Follow the road to reach a junction and, soon after, a stile on the right. Cross the stile and bear half-left across the field beyond, heading towards a slightly higher wooden fencing. Cross the railway, again with care, and follow the clear track beyond, crossing Mill Beck, to reach the A166, Turn left and follow the pavement to return to Burton Agnes. Turn left along the footpath immediately before the pond to return to the start.

POINTS OF INTEREST:

Burton Agnes – Burton Agnes Hall is open to the public and contains much of interest.
Rudston Roam – This is the third of the linking series of four 20 mile walks, the Roam going from Driffield to Bridlington.
Woldgate – This Roman road linked York to Bridlington. Views from it include the cranes of the Hull docks and the cooling towers at Saltend. Rudston Beacon is a little to the right of where the route first meets the road.
Rudston – In the churchyard is the Rudston Monolith, reputed to be the tallest standing stone in England. The grave of author Winifred Holtby, and the resting place of the Lord MacDonalds of the Isles can also be found. A Roman villa stood nearby.

REFRESHMENTS:

The Bluebell Inn, opposite the Rudston Road, Burton Agnes, has given excellent service to Rudston Roam walkers.
The Bosville Arms, Rudston.

Maps: OS Sheets Landranger 107; Pathfinder 676.
Gentle walking through pleasant countryside mainly along green lanes and field paths.
Start: At 163466, on Breamer Lane, Seaton.

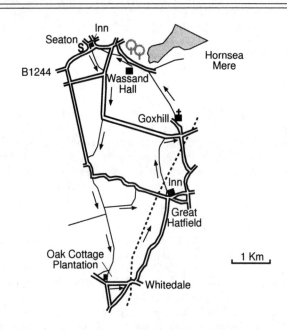

From Breamer Lane, turn left along Main Street and, close to the bend and before the Sun Inn, turn right down Butcher Row. Now follow a footpath which goes through a gate and a garden to reach a stile. Go over and bear slightly right, downhill, to reach a second stile in the corner of the small field. Go over and straight ahead across the field beyond, heading slightly to the right of a telegraph pole, to reach a hedge. Walk half-left from here, heading towards a gap in the hedge. Turn right along the lane beyond, then keep ahead along the road reached at a corner, following it to a sharp left-hand bend.

At the bend, go ahead along wide, grassy Green Lane which soon bears right to reach a road. Turn left and, at the next sharp bend, go ahead along the equally grassy Folly Lane. Go past a bridleway junction on the left (an easy short cut to Great Hatfield) and then pass a junction with a bridleway to Rise, on the right, continuing to reach the Rise to Hornsea road at Oak Cottages (at a road junction). Turn left along the Hornsea road to reach Whitedale. Here, turn left along the old **Hull to Hornsea railway** and follow it to the road by the remains of Sigglesthorne station. Turn right to reach Great Hatfield and the Wrygarth Arms Inn.

Take the footpath which runs between the inn and a house to reach an open field. Keep ahead, with trees on your right, and cross a stile to regain the old railway. Turn right for a short distance then, at the end of a group of taller bushes, descend to reach a plank bridge. Cross and ascend the field beyond. Now go along a footpath, bearing right, with a hedge on your right. Cross a small bridge over a drain and continue along the drain side. Cross a footbridge on the right and then walk with a smaller drain on your right. Continue ahead to reach the road to Goxhill.

Turn right to reach a crossroads. Turn left into Goxhill and walk to **St Giles' Church**. A footpath alongside the church goes through a gate and maintains direction, crossing to the far left corner of a field, with a pond on your left, to reach a gap. Go through the gap, walk along a short track and walk ahead along a narrow grass path to reach a slightly hidden stile. Go over and head half-right across the next field to reach a small section of wooden fencing. Cross, if possible. If not, divert to the gate in the right-hand corner. Cross the next field to reach a stile to the right of taller trees and cross to the far right-hand field corner to reach a track. Turn left and go past the entry to Home Farm, close to **Wassand Hall**. Just before reaching a lodge, at the start of a track on the left, find a narrow footpath between trees and follow it to a stile. Go over and cross a field to the left of a pond to reach the B1244. Turn left, with care, to return to Seaton.

POINTS OF INTEREST:

Hull to Hornsea Railway – The line is now a bridleway from the outskirts of Hull to Hornsea. There is a small Nature Reserve near Hatfield.

St Giles' Church – This fine old church is well worth a look inside.

Wassand Hall – The Hall is at the centre of the estate this walk passes through. Hornsea Mere, adjoining the Hall, is easily reached by footpath.

REFRESHMENTS:
The Sun Inn, Seaton.
The Wrygarth Arms, Hatfield.

Walk 92   KIRBY UNDERDALE   9m (14½km)

Maps: OS Sheets Landranger 106; Pathfinder 666.

Lovely Wolds scenery, taking in dry grassy valleys and old tracks. Some moderately hard climbing to the highest part of the Wolds.

Start: At 835567, the picnic site off the A166 to the west of Fridaythorpe.

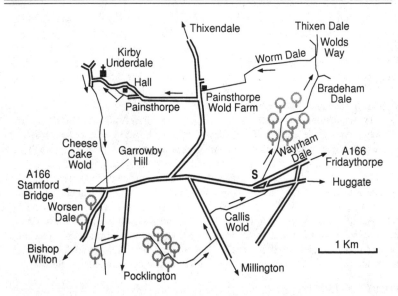

From the car park go to the western end of the picnic site and cross the A166, with care, to take the track opposite down into Wayrham Dale. Follow the track, soon going through a plantation, to a dale junction. There, bear right, through Bradeham Dale, and go past a dew pond to reach another dale junction. Cross the stile and bear left into Thixen Dale. Ahead, the Wolds Way descends a chalk track into the dale, but, before reaching the bottom, turn left up the smaller Worm Dale to reach a grass track angling across the dale. Bear left, uphill, along this. Near the top, go to the right of a dew pond and then through a gateway in the field corner. Follow the path ahead, with a hedge on your left and soon, at a field corner, turn left to join a farm track. Follow the track, bearing right to reach a road by Painsthorpe Wold Farm.

Turn left along the road and then right at a junction, descending Painsthorpe Lane. At Painsthorpe, go down the 'No Through Road', bearing right at its end to go along a grass track. Cross a stile on the right, just before a bend, and go across the field beyond, heading towards **All Saints' Church** at Kirby Underdale. Cross a stile and turn left along the road to reach the church.

Now go uphill now, past a war memorial, to reach a T-junction. Turn left, go through a gate – beware of mud, – and follow the main track as it ascends, fairly steeply in parts, through gates and over Cheese Cake Wold to reach the A166 again, close to the top of **Garrowby Hill**. Cross the road, with care, and descend along the Bishop Wilton road to reach a plantation. Now find the narrow path on the left, following it, with a slight scramble, uphill. (A diversion can be made down the road to the Fleece Inn at Bishop Wilton, but this results in a hard climb along a waymarked footpath.)

The path turns right, with excellent views, and then turns left and uphill as it reaches a plantation. Go over a stile by a gate to join the path up from Bishop Wilton. Continue ahead, uphill, along a grass track to reach a road. Cross the road and go through a gate to continue along a track. Descend the track, bearing right, through woodland into **Deep Dale**. Go past a track on the left and, soon, reach a footpath opposite a small hut. Take this, descending steeply.

Cross the stile at the bottom and ascend the steep, grassy slope ahead, bearing left, away from Deep Dale, towards the end of a line of bushes. Turn left along the grass track reached at the top and go through gates to reach a road. Turn left and follow the road to reach a track on the right. Follow this, going through two gates and then following the line of the hedge on the right to reach the field corner. Go a little distance to the left to reach a stile, cross and descend the path beyond to reach the road close to the picnic site.

POINTS OF INTEREST:

All Saints' Church – This is a lovely old church in a very pleasant setting. It is the burial place of the Halifax family from the Garrowby Estate.

Garrowby Hill – The long climb up to Cheese Cake Wold ends at the top of the hill. The highest point of the Wolds lies at nearby Cot Nab.

Deep Dale – This is a pleasant, partly wooded valley. The climb out may seem a little hard.

REFRESHMENTS:

None en route, but as noted a diversion can be made to the *Fleece Inn*, Bishop Wilton. Fridaythorpe, with an inn and a restaurant, is also not far distant.

Walk 93   BARDNEY AND SOUTHREY   9¹/₄m (14³/₄km)

Maps: OS Sheets Landranger 121; Pathfinders 765 and 782.

A level walk visiting two medieval abbey sites.

Start: At 120694, Church Lane, Bardney.

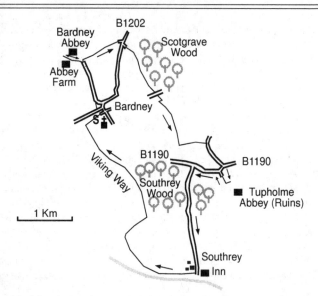

Bardney straddles the B1190 east of Lincoln. There is a small parking area between the green and the church.

Walk to **Bardney** village green and turn left. Turn left again into Station Road, cross into an alleyway by W S Smith and Sons and join Abbey Road, keep left and follow it to a bridleway on the right by a brick water tower. Continue ahead to the site of **Bardney Abbey** (behind Abbey Farm) then return and take the bridleway. At a road, turn right for 50 yards, then go left along a green lane, following it to the far end of Scotgrave Wood. Cross a stile and walk beside a wire fence to a handgate. Go through, and continue through a farmyard to reach a road. Cross and take a track past a house. Take the second waymarked path on the left, near a large warehouse, and follow the field edge. Cross a footbridge, go ahead over another field to reach a stile in a wire fence and then aim to the left of the nearby farm where a stile leads to a lane.

Turn right to a T-junction and turn right again to **Tupholme Abbey**. After exploring, turn left at the exit along the road, and left again at the sign for **Southrey**. Follow this quiet road through the village to reach the bank of River Witham. Turn right along the old railway track beside the river. This soon veers to the right, away from the riverbank, becoming enclosed by trees. About a mile from Southrey, take the second prominent track to the right. Turn left at the junction with another track near the corner of Southrey Wood, this is the Viking Way, and, ignoring side tracks, continue to the edge of Bardney. Now watch for a footpath on the right which runs behind houses to join Church Lane. Walk past the church to return to the start.

POINTS OF INTEREST:

Bardney – The name comes from *Bearda* a Saxon landowner and *Ey* meaning island. Attractive buildings surround the green, the oldest being the 15th-century church. Nearby is a hospital founded by a Peter Hancock in 1712, the date prominent in Roman numerals, and the Kitchings Charity school of 1843. A modern addition is a memorial, with a large aircraft propeller, to the 9th Squadron Royal Air Force who were stationed at Bardney airfield.

Bardney Abbey – Founded by King Ethelred circa 675AD, this was the shrine of King (and Saint) Oswald, Ethelred's uncle. Only Oswald's body rested here, his head being at Lindisfarne and his arms at Bamburgh. Sacked by the Danes in 870, Bardney was refounded 200 years later, but dissolved by Henry VIII in 1538 after the Lincolnshire Rising in which some monks participated. From 1909 to 1915 the local vicar, Rev Charles Laing, excavated the site. Much stonework was revealed, but in 1933 it was covered for protection from the weather.

Tupholme Abbey – The name comes partly from *tups*, meaning sheep, an indication of land use before the abbey was founded in 1155. Tupholme lasted less than 400 years. Dissolved in 1536, it has since been a farmhouse, and there was even a pop festival here in 1972. Only part of the refectory remains. Display boards give a detailed history, explaining the monks way of life, and describing the natural history: the site is a Nature Reserve.

Southrey – The unusual church, built of wood in 1898, has the colonial appearance of some far-flung corner of the empire. Note the magnificent weathercock. At one time there was a regular ferry across the Witham here.

REFRESHMENTS:
The Bards Inn, Bardney.
The Nags Head, Bardney.
The Riverside Inn, Southrey.

Walk 94　　THE HEATH AND TEMPLE BRUER　　9¹/₂m (15¹/₄km)

Maps: OS Sheets Landranger 121; Pathfinders 797 and 798.

*An exhilarating, but easy, walk over the Heath to a medieval
Knights' Templar preceptory.*

Start: At 983566, the church, Hall Street, Wellingore.

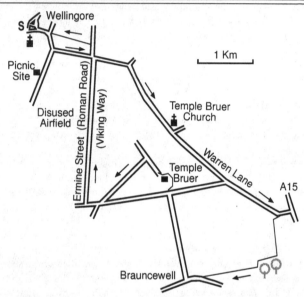

Walk away from the church and, at the edge of the village, turn right along Pottergate.
At a junction, turn left, then continue forwards when a crossroads is reached. Follow
the quiet road to **Temple Bruer Church** (at grid reference 010547), then keep straight
ahead along the unmade track of **Warren Lane**. Where this joins a road, continue
ahead until a left-hand bend is reached. There, double back sharply to the right to go
along a field edge with a stone wall on your right. After 100 yards, turn left and follow
a clear headland path to a line of trees on the horizon. Turn right and, at the end of the
trees, continue in the same direction towards a grey farmhouse, walking along a field
headland with a boundary wall on your right. Keep forward at a gate to reach a road at
the edge of **Brauncewell**. Turn right, walk through the village and take the track on the
right by Grange Farm. Follow the track to **Temple Bruer** 1 mile away. Cross the road

and follow the signs to the remains of the preceptory behind the main farm buildings. Leaving the tower, turn left, then right to continue from the rear of the farmyard, passing two white cottages. Turn left at a track junction on to a wide grass track and follow this to a road.

Turn right and, after 300 yards, turn right again. Now head northwards along the Roman **Ermine Street** (part of the Viking Way), passing **Wellingore Airfield** to cross the outward route at grid reference 995561. Keep ahead for another 200 yards, then turn left along a field path, aiming for Wellingore church. Cross Pottergate and walk back into Wellingore.

POINTS OF INTEREST:

Temple Bruer Church – The church was built in 1874 by the Lincolnshire architect James Fowler.

Warren Lane – As its name suggests, this was where the medieval rabbit warrens were situated. In the early 1800s there may have been up to 100 acres of them.

Brauncewell – The village has a Horse Gin, essentially a horse-powered threshing machine, using four horses tethered to an overhead beam. Gears were driven by the animals who walked around a circular track. The restored building is to the left as you walk through the village.

Temple Bruer – All that remains now of this 12th-century preceptory is the south tower. The Knights' Templar were an order of warrior monks formed after the crusades to protect pilgrims. Temple Bruer was their second richest property in the country: at one time there were 37 tenant farmers and a market. Information boards at the site give a detailed history. Admission is free and graffiti is rife, going back over many years: the oldest found by the author dates from 1689.

Ermine Street – This was the main Roman road from London to York. The route went via Stamford and Lincoln, with a ferry over the Humber.

Wellingore Airfield – The airfield originated in 1917 as a naval landing ground. It was much enlarged in 1940. Guy Gibson, later of 'Dambusters' fame, spent some time here with 29 Squadron, lodging in Navenby. In 1945 it became a camp for German and Ukrainian prisoners of war and was sold for farmland again in the 1950s. An information board is passed on the walk at grid reference 994549.

REFRESHMENTS:

The Marquis of Granby, High Street, Wellingore.

The Red Lion, High Street, Wellingore.

There is also a picnic site and viewpoint on part of the old airfield, off Pottergate at grid reference 984555.

Maps: OS Sheets Landranger 112; Pathfinders 717 and 728.
*Fine views of the 'island' of Axholme, home to the Wesleys and
the Haxey Hood Game.*
Start: At 783039, Kings Head Croft car park, Epworth.

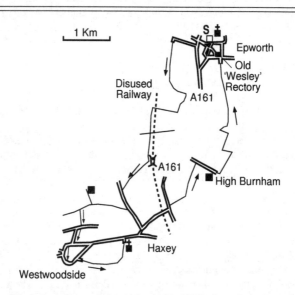

The Isle of Axholme rises only to some 130ft (40m), but gives distant views in all
directions. The car park is off the Market Place, near the church.

From the car park turn right and walk down to High Street and the traffic lights. Turn
left, and then first right into Fieldside. At the end, turn left into Stud Cross. Continue
along a track and, when this splits three ways, take the left-hand branch towards a hill.
Join another track, turn right up the hill, and, at the top, go right, down the far side, to
another junction. Turn right to reach the old **Axholme Railway**. Turn left along the old
trackbed, now a Nature Reserve. A culvert must be negotiated because the bridge has
gone, and, at a lane where another bridge is missing, you must descend to the right to
reach the other side. At a brick bridge parapet, descend the embankment on the right
on to a farm track. Turn right to reach a road. Turn left for 150 yards, then right along

a signed track, bearing right at the top along a farm road. When this goes down to the farm, keep straight on for 300 yards, then take a footpath on the left: the sign and stile are set back in a tiny valley. Turn right when you reach a road and, on reaching Gollands Lane, go left. At the bottom, cross to the path opposite, and, at an old chapel by a road junction, follow Sandbeds Lane opposite. In a few yards, bear right along a track, following it until it curves leftwards uphill to **Haxey** church.

Turn right and, in the village, go left up Green Hill to reach the A161. Turn left for 30 yards, then cross, with care, to go along a wide green lane. Take the first grass track on the left and, at a road, turn right. Beyond High Burnham Farm, go left opposite the pond. The track becomes a headland path leading down to the field corner: turn left and, shortly, right at a waymarker. With a ditch on your left, walk to another track. Turn left, but almost at once, right along another headland to reach a dyke: there is a crossing point to your right. Walk back on the other side to a copse and do a right U-turn (near waymarkers) on to the track beyond it. At a hedge, turn left, uphill, along a headland. From the field corner, go straight across the next field on to a final headland. This merges with a track, reaching Epworth opposite **The Old Rectory**. Turn left, then right down Albion Hill to return to the Market Place.

POINTS OF INTEREST:

Axholme Railway – This branch line was only open from 1905 to 1965. Now a Nature Reserve it provides a habitat for many plants (including orchids), birds and butterflies.

Haxey – On the 6th January each year, regardless of the weather, Haxey is the scene of the Hood Game. Almost the entire male populations of Haxey and neighbouring Westwoodside fight for possession of the 'hood' and attempt to secure it in their own pub. The melee begins at mid-day and may last several hours. The game is thought to have originated in the 13th century when Lady de Mowbray lost a scarf and farm labourers scrambled to return it. Complicated preliminaries and rules involve a 'Lord', a 'Fool', ten 'Boggins' and a 'Chief Boggin'.

The Old Rectory – This was the home of Rev Samuel Wesley and his wife Susannah from 1696 to 1735, and here John and Charles Wesley were born in 1703 and 1708. Both ardent preachers, they travelled the length and breadth of the country and founded the Wesleyan Methodist Church. The original rectory burned down in 1709 when John nearly lost his life. It is open to the public between March and October.

REFRESHMENTS:

The Duke William, Haxey.
The Red Lion, Epworth.
The Tiny Teapot Café, Epworth.

Walk 96   ALKBOROUGH AND WEST HALTON   9³/₄m (15¹/₂km)

Maps: OS Sheets Landranger 112; Pathfinders 695 and 706.

Magnificent river views and a medieval maze.

Start: At 869187, Burton Hills car park and picnic site.

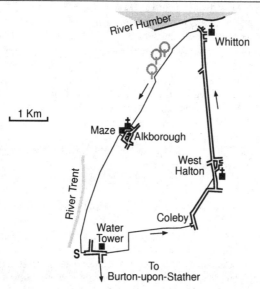

Drive north from Scunthorpe on the B1430. The picnic site is down the track on the left to 'The Cliff', just beyond Burton Stather village.

Return to the road and walk ahead to a right-hand bend. Take the track by the water tower, ignoring side tracks for 750 yards, to reach a belt of trees. Here, a waymarker directs you to the left. Walk to the field corner, turn right and follow another track to the road near Coleby. Turn left through **Coleby** and when the road bends right, go forward on a signposted fieldpath. (If the soil has recently been tilled you will almost certainly find fossils here.) Cross two stiles and a paddock to regain the road opposite a house. Turn left to **West Halton**. (For the Butchers Arms go right into Churchside and down West Street.)

The route follows the road to Whitton. There are wide verges, but it is virtually traffic free, and the views over the **Humber** become increasingly impressive, with the

182

Humber Bridge visible to the right. When you are level with Whitton Church, take the signed footpath over a stile on the left and walk to another stile on the skyline. The path beyond dips towards the river but, at a waymarker, contours away to the left along the grass slope. Just before some woods, cross a stile in the hedge on your left and turn right to continue behind the woods. At a field corner, go around the end of a high hedge, then continue in the original direction. Cross a stile and keep forward along the hilltop, going through woods and over a stony lane (with a stile and steps on both sides) into another field. Cross a metalled lane to another stile, then head for **Alkborough Church**, reaching it after crossing another lane and going up a grassy ramp. Walk to the right of the church, into Churchside, and go right again into **Julian's Bower** maze. Take the path to the left of the maze and, ignoring all side tracks and paths, walk along the top of 'The Cliff' for almost 2 miles, with the River Trent below you. At a cross-path signpost, turn left to the start.

POINTS OF INTEREST:

Coleby – The local rocks are Jurassic, 135 million years old, and rich in fossils. As you pass through the village inspect the barn walls.

West Halton – Near the church porch is a small, but unusual, war memorial to 'The Sons and Brothers' of Women's Institute members. It incorporates a tap!

The Humber – This huge river estuary, starting near Alkborough at the confluence of the Ouse and the Trent, is clearly and spectacularly seen from the path.

Alkborough Church – A church site for 800 years and steeped in history. During restoration in 1887 skeletons found beneath the floor were believed to be the remains of Cavalier soldiers killed in the church at the Battle of Alkborough during the Civil War. Near the tower, lifting a ring-stone reveals some Roman masonry. The carved reredos, installed in 1920, is by the famous 'Mousey' Thompson and bears his usual mouse trademark. In the centre of the east window, and in the floor of the porch, are copies of the nearby maze. (Practice your route before you get to the real thing!) Outside, the church cross has been worn away through use as a sharpener for swords, scythes and arrows.

Julian's Bower – The maze is 44 ft across. An early theory that it was a Roman game, brought from Troy by Julius, accounts for its popular name. It is now considered to be about 800 years old and to have been created by monks who may have walked it with pebbles in their shoes as a penance.

REFRESHMENTS:
The Butchers Arms, West Halton.
The Sheffield Arms, Burton-upon-Stather.

Walk 97   GRIMSTHORPE CASTLE   10m (16km)

Maps: OS Sheets Landranger 130; Pathfinder 856 and 877.
The park of Grimsthorpe Castle and the surrounding villages.
Start: At 062218 in Edenham. Park with care off the main road.

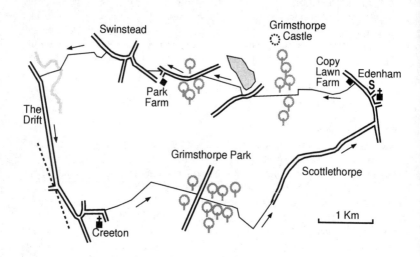

From Edenham head towards Grimsthorpe, then turn left into Copy Lawn Farm.
Beyond the gate at the end of the farmyard, go right, crossing two fields. Cross a stile
and follow the path up the field edge towards woods. Go left, to round the corner of the
woods, then go through a narrow strip of woodland ahead. Go downhill beside a wire
fence to reach a gate, with marvellous views of the lake, park and **Grimsthorpe Castle**.
From the gate, go slightly right, to reach an estate road. Keeping the lake-shore on your
right, leave the road and walk around to the outfall. Now follow a track which rises
leftwards towards the skyline. Go left along a wider track until you are level with Park
Farm then, next to a track junction, cross a stile on the left and walk towards the
buildings of **Swinstead** seen ahead. Join a farm access road down to the village and turn
left for the Windmill Inn.

    Leave along the Corby Glen road, then, near where the houses end, take a
signposted track on the left. Follow a path over a stile on the right, bearing left around
a hedge corner to reach a second stile. Now stay with the hedge and, after 200 yards,

cross a stile on the left. Descend half-right into the valley, going left to cross a bridge over the West Glen river. From a stile near the corner of some woods, walk uphill to reach 'The Drift', a wide green lane. Turn left and follow this, and a minor road, to reach the B1176 at **Creeton**. (Do not go under the **railway**.)

Turn left and, after 150 yards, turn right, by the river, along a 'No Through Road'. Where this bends right, climb the stile on the left, (but first detour to the church) and ascend the field beyond, walking parallel to the hedge/fence on your right. In the top corner, go through a gate and along the edges of two more fields. In the third, go right at a waymarked handgate and follow a grassy track to reach a tarmac road. Go straight over and follow a path to the far edge of the woods. The path bends right to skirt the trees before bending left across a field to join a farm track. Turn left and follow the track, which becomes tarmac for almost 2 miles, through Scottlethorpe, to return to **Edenham**.

POINTS OF INTEREST:

Grimsthorpe Castle – The castle is the seat of the Dukes of Ancaster. Begun in the 13th century and culminating in the work of Van Brugh in 1722, the castle has evolved into the present magnificent building. It is sometimes open to the public. In the valley to the south there was a 12th-century Cistercian abbey known then as Vallis Dei, but since corrupted to The Vaudy.

Swinstead – Just before entering Swinstead, a Summer House, also designed by Van Brugh, can be seen. The village still has the remains of its stone market cross.

Creeton – There are fragments of Saxon crosses in the beautiful church on the hillside. Look, too, for the poetic gravestone of Clement Nidd near the chancel.

The Edenham to Little Bytham Railway – Lord Willoughby d'Eresby built a branch line, linking with the Great Northern, in 1855. It was unsuccessful and closed in 1880. Its line can be clearly seen on the map, and 'on the ground' near the end of the walk at Scottlethorpe. Copy Lawn Farm was the terminus.

Edenham – The church, overshadowed by enormous cedar trees, contains monuments to the Willoughby d'Eresby family (the Dukes of Ancaster) and a small brass, reputedly of St Thomas of Canterbury, rescued from a niche in the tower. Legend has it that Henry VIII's men could not reach it because they did not have a long enough ladder. Charles Kingsley reputedly wrote *Hereward the Wake* in the vicarage.

REFRESHMENTS:

The Five Bells, Edenham.
The Windmill Inn, Swinstead.

Walk 98 BISCATHORPE AND BURGH-ON-BAIN 10m (16km)

Maps: OS Sheets Landranger 122; Pathfinder 748.

A delightful Wolds walk to five 'lost' medieval villages.

Start: At 229849, Biscathorpe, near the fords by the church.

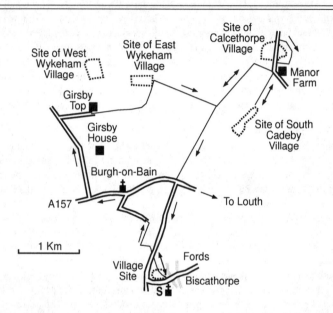

Cross the River Bain by the footbridge and go uphill to a stile near the left corner of some woods, going through to reach a lane. Cross the stile opposite and follow a fieldpath to a second stile, turning left downhill by a fence. Turn right beside the River Bain following it to an old mill. Cross the bridge and take a track towards Burgh-on-Bain. Turn right up Mill Lane to reach the A157.

Turn left along the pavement for 500 yards to reach a lane on the right for Girsby. Cross, with care, and follow the lane past the gateway to Girsby House. Take the next lane on the right. From it West Wykeham village can be glimpsed on the far side of the valley. There is no public right of way to it however. The lane passes Girsby Top and becomes a track bending leftwards downhill to reach a green gate by a cottage. Go through and continue for 100 yards to reach the next cottage. The remains of East Wykeham village are on your left here. Turn right along a bridleway, following it to a three-way footpath signpost at 238879.

To return directly to Biscathorpe from here, turn right. However, the main route continues to two further **village sites**: turn left, soon bearing right with the track to reach a road near Calcethorpe Manor. Turn left and walk to the second access stile on the right, beyond a derelict house. On your left here are just some of the extensive remains of Calcethorpe. Cross the stile, turn half-right and head for a footbridge. Continue towards another stile with a white arrow. Ridge and furrow fields, and village remains now surround you: go half-right up to another white arrow on the skyline. Turn right towards a farm, bearing right again to go through a gate. Turn left, past a pond, to reach the first access stile passed earlier. Reverse the outward route along the road and, as it bends left go straight ahead on a track by the white house for $^1/_2$ mile to reach the site of South Candleby. Now reverse the route back to the signpost at GR 238879.

Continue southwards along the track to reach the A157. Cross, with great care, and follow the lane opposite to rejoin the outward route above **Biscathorpe**. Retrace your steps to your car.

POINTS OF INTEREST:

Lost Medieval Villages – The reasons why the villages were abandoned are in many instances unclear. The plague arrived in Britain in 1348 and ravaged Lincolnshire in the years 1349 and 1350. However, historians now believe that the Black Death was only one cause of depopulation. Other reasons, including famine, economic changes, new farming practices, such as the emphasis on sheep, all played their part, and, of course, these factors varied in their impact from place to place.

And the fifth lost village? You passed over it on the grass slopes when leaving and returning to Biscathorpe footbridge.

Biscathorpe – A picturesque spot with two fords and a little Victorian church dedicated to St Helen who, legend has it, discovered part of the Cross upon which Jesus was crucified. Check (with amazement) the scale of old charges for burials etc.

REFRESHMENTS:

None en route, though there is a small shop at Burgh-on-Bain. The nearest are at Ludford, 3 miles to the north, or Donington-on-Bain, 2 miles to the south.

Walk 99   NETTLETON AND ROTHWELL   10m (16km)

Maps: OS Sheets Landranger 113; Pathfinder 719 and 730.

A strenuous walk, including deep valleys and Lincolnshire's highest 'wold'.

Start: At 109002, the Salutation Inn, Nettleton.

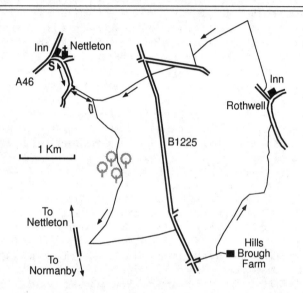

Turn off the A46 by the Salutation Inn at Nettleton. There is a small lay-by near the village stores. (Alternatively park in the lane leading to Normanby – at about GR 112996 – and join the route at the lane to Nettleton Grange.)

Walk away from the A46, keeping right at the first junction. Now, where the road bends right, go left along a lane, waymarked as part of the Viking Way, heading towards Nettleton Grange. Cross the commemorative stile for the Nev Cole Way (*see* Note to Walk 71) and turn right. Pass to the left of a pond and above some scrubland, then gradually descend to the right to reach a wire fence near a stream. Proceed up **Nettleton Valley**. Go over a footbridge and two stiles to reach a quarry road. Turn left for a few yards, then right into woodland. Go down some steps and through a tunnel, then, at a gate and stile, veer slightly right to rejoin the stream and wire fence. When the fence ends, continue uphill to join a farm track, which crosses the head of the valley. You will have climbed a fair height by now, but with the reward of far reaching views. Turn left along the track, which soon becomes a headland path. At this point you are just below **Normanby Top**, a field away to your right. Maintain direction to reach a bridlegate at Caistor High Street (the B1225).

Turn right along the wide grass verge to reach the entrance to Hills Brough Farm. Turn left along its access road and, after 400 yards, in a pronounced hollow, turn left again. The farmer's sign says 'Footpath – follow the Valley': do just that, following your 'nose' down and along the valley bottom until you reach another surfaced farm road. Turn right along this, passing some ponds to reach a road. Turn left into Rothwell. Turn left, go past the inn and then turn right into Wold View. Keep left, making a long gradual climb along a surfaced track before leaving it at a bend by a telegraph pole. Continue ahead along a grass track but, at a hedge, with a cross-path and waymarkers, turn left along a path which becomes a track. When it joins another, keep left to reach a road. Turn right along a bridleway on the 'inside' of a high hedge, walking parallel to the road to reach a prominent gap. Go through, cross the road and take the continuing bridleway by turning sharp right beyond the hedge on the opposite side. When High Street (the B1225) is reached, go straight over and follow the track opposite, going downhill to reach the Nev Cole stile crossed earlier. Retrace your outward route to the Salutation Inn.

POINTS OF INTEREST:

Nettleton Valley – Perhaps the most dramatic valley in the Wolds. Beneath its slopes iron ore was once mined for Lysaght's steelworks in Scunthorpe. Activity began in 1929 and during the mine's history both opencast and underground mining took place. A railway first tunnelled into the ridge to the west of the valley, but by the 1950s increased demand meant that tunnels were driven into the eastern hillside too, hence the embankment and foot tunnel through which the path passes. Peak annual production was over a quarter of a million tons in 1967. The mine closed in 1969 and the opencast area has been restored.

Normanby Top – This is the highest point in Lincolnshire at 550 feet (168 metres). The triangulation pillar marking it is only a few yards to the south of the path to High Street. The radar scanner belongs to the Civil Aviation Authority.

REFRESHMENTS:

The Salutation Inn, Nettleton.
The Nickerson Arms, Rothwell.
There are also facilities in Caistor.

Maps: OS Sheets Landranger 122; Pathfinder 766 and 783.
A Roman town, a deer park, a disused railway and a canal.
Start: At 263695, the Tourist Information Centre, Horncastle.

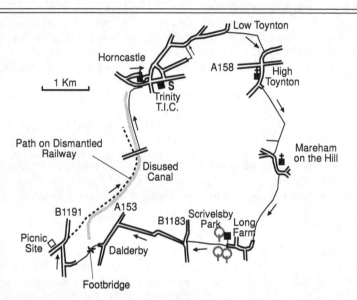

From the TIC, Spilsby Road, **Horncastle**, go along Stanhope Road opposite, turning right into Bowl Alley Lane. Beyond the school, a footpath veers right from the road. Follow it to a road and turn right for Low Toynton. Keep right at the fork and then take the track on the right, near the post-box, bearing right to reach a minor road. Turn right to reach the main A158. Cross, with care, and go along the lane by the church. Now take the bridleway on the left, but, at some houses, leave the farm track, going left, uphill, along a grass path. Go through a transport yard to reach a road in Mareham-on-the-Hill. Turn left. (After 200 yards the church is tucked away, by a pond, up a grassy lane.)

Walk out of the village and, just after a left bend, turn right along a green lane, following it for 1$^1/_4$ miles to reach a metalled road. Keep straight ahead, following the road to Long Farm. Go over an area of rough grass and through two gates, the second in a deer fence, to reach **Scrivelsby Park**. Continue ahead across the park to reach the B1183. Turn left, then right along a lane signed to **Dalderby**. When the lane reaches the A153, turn left along the wide grass verge. At Dalderby turn right along the lane near the War Memorial. Go through a gate and continue to a footbridge over the River Bain and a disused lock over the **Horncastle Canal**.

Continue across a pasture to the far right corner to join a green lane, following it to a minor road. Turn right to reach the B1191 (to Woodhall Spa). Turn left for a few yards to reach a car park and picnic site on the right, by the old railway. Turn sharp right along the old trackbed, going under a bridge and continuing for $1^1/_4$ miles to reach Thornton Lodge. Turn right, cross the canal, and then turn left along its bank into Horncastle. Go right, past the swimming pool, and walk to a pedestrian crossing on the left. Cross the road and the river. (The library with its Roman wall is along to your right.) Go up Church Lane, bear right through the Market Place, go right again in the Bullring, and then left at the traffic lights to return to the start.

POINTS OF INTEREST:

Horncastle – The town site has been occupied for 8,000 years. The Roman town lay between the Rivers Bain and Waring. A section of Roman wall is preserved in the library. There was much activity during the Civil War when Cromwell won a decisive victory at nearby Winceby in 1643. Famous for its horse fair, by 1814 the largest in Britain, Horncastle attracted dealers, aristocracy, even crown princes, from all over this country, Europe, Russia and America. George Borrow, in *Romany Rye* tells of his adventures, and profits made, at Horncastle in 1857. The fair dwindled rapidly in this century ending in 1948.

In Church Lane a macabre plaque marks the shop of William Marwood, a 19th-century cobbler and executioner, who invented the 'long drop' method of hanging.

Scrivelsby Park – The Court is the home of the Dymoke family, the traditional Champions of England, whose duty was to ride into coronation ceremonies challenging all-comers in single combat on the monarchs behalf. In the Park you will almost certainly see some deer.

Dalderby – The war memorial commemorates eleven volunteers in the Great War, from a population then barely twice that number. Thankfully ten came back.

The Horncastle Canal and Railway – The canal was dug in 1810, construction from the Witham taking 14 years. Walking by it now it is hard to imagine 50 ton boats (14ft by 72ft) using it. There were connections to Nottingham, Leeds and Manchester. A return trip to Boston took 4 days. The canal closed in 1878, the railway having arrived in 1855. This in its turn closed in 1971.

REFRESHMENTS:

There are several possibilities in Horncastle.

Titles in the Series